ENGLISH LANGUAGE TESTING IN U.S. COLLEGES AND UNIVERSITIES

Edited by Dan Douglas

National Association for
Foreign Student Affairs
Washington, DC

The National Association for Foreign Student Affairs (NAFSA) is a nonprofit membership organization that provides training, information, and other educational services to professionals in the field of international educational exchange. Its 6,100 members—from every state in the United States and more than 50 other countries—make it the largest professional membership association in the world concerned with the advancement of effective international educational exchange. Members represent primarily colleges and universities but also elementary and secondary schools, public and private educational associations, exchange organizations, national and international corporations and foundations, and community organizations. Through its publications, workshops, consultations with institutions, and conferences, the association serves as a source of professional training, a reference for standards of performance, and an advocate for the most effective operation of international educational exchange.

Support for this publication was provided by the Advising, Teaching, and Specialized Programs Division of the U.S. Information Agency.

Copies of this publication may be ordered from the Publications Order Desk, National Association for Foreign Student Affairs, 1860 19th Street, N.W., Washington, D.C. 20009

Library of Congress Cataloging-in-Publication Data

English language testing in U.S. colleges and universities / edited by Dan Douglas.
    p.   cm.
    Includes bibliographical references.
    ISBN 0-912207-56-6
    1. English language—Foreign Speakers—Ability testing.
    2. English language—Study and teaching (Higher)—Foreign speakers.
    3. English language—Study and teaching (Higher)—United States.
    4. Universities and colleges—United States—Examinations.
    I. Douglas, Dan.
    PE1128.A2E54   1990
    428'.0076—dc20   90-36384
                                                                                               CIP

© 1990 by the National Association for Foreign Student Affairs.
All rights reserved. Printed in the United States of America.

Contents

	PREFACE	v
1	OVERVIEW OF ESL TESTING *Ralph Pat Barrett*	1
2	ENGLISH LANGUAGE TESTING: THE VIEW FROM THE ADMISSIONS OFFICE *G. James Haas*	9
3	ENGLISH LANGUAGE TESTING: THE VIEW FROM THE ENGLISH TEACHING PROGRAM *Paul J. Angelis*	19
4	STANDARDIZED ESL TESTS USED IN U.S. COLLEGES AND UNIVERSITIES *Harold S. Madsen*	27
5	BRITISH TESTS OF ENGLISH AS A FOREIGN LANGUAGE *J. Charles Alderson*	41
6	ESL COMPOSITION TESTING *Jane Hughey*	51
7	THE TESTING AND EVALUATION OF INTERNATIONAL TEACHING ASSISTANTS *Barbara S. Plakans and Roberta G. Abraham*	68
8	INTERPRETING TEST SCORES *Grant Henning*	82
	REFERENCES	91
	Appendix A Addresses for Information on English Language Testing	95
	Appendix B ESL Composition Test Questionnaire	97

Preface

This book is intended for those working with international students on U.S. college and university campuses who need to better understand testing practices and uses, and the meaning of English language test scores. Admissions officers, international student counsellors and advisers, and instructors in intensive English programs, remedial English as a second language (ESL) courses, or freshman composition courses will find information about the need for English language tests, the types of tests available, the establishment of testing and evaluation programs, and the interpretation of test results.

The book has been written for people whose primary interest is in making correct decisions about the admission, placement, and instruction of international students, rather than for people whose primary interest is in English language testing itself. Therefore, technical jargon, theoretical issues, and statistical intricacies have been kept to a minimum. The aim has been to provide a sensible and practical reference work that can be consulted rapidly by those who need information about a particular problem, or read through when the goal is to obtain a fuller picture of language testing practice.

The book begins with an overview of English language testing in U.S. colleges and universities by Ralph Pat Barrett, of Michigan State University. He outlines the major considerations in the testing and evaluation of the English language skills of international students: the functions of testing, the types of tests, and the strengths and limitations of language tests. This introductory chapter is followed by one written by a university admissions officer with more than 20 years' experience in the evaluation of international applications. G. James Haas, of Indiana University, though not a language testing expert, writes in a pragmatic manner of the concerns, problems, and practices of admissions officers in dealing appropriately with information about the English language skills of international applicants.

He considers the setting of admission standards, some unreliable sources of information on English language proficiency, the interpretation of standard score reports (such as those from Educational Testing Service or the University of Michigan English Language Institute), and problems with unusual reports, such as some from outside the United States. Haas provides specific, down-to-earth advice in such areas as allowing for margins of error in Test of English as a Foreign Language (TOEFL) scores, using a rule-of-thumb for converting Michigan Test Battery scores to a TOEFL scale, and dealing with applicants who submit no English language test scores at all. In Chapter Three, Paul J. Angelis, of Southern Illinois University, takes a pragmatic approach, in much the same vein as Haas, in discussing specific issues for on-campus English language testing concerning the placement of students in intensive English programs, remedial ESL classes, or non-ESL university classes. He considers the problems of deciding who should be tested on campus, which language skills need to be tested, and how a testing program can be structured.

Chapters Four and Five contain critical overviews of standardized English language tests available in the United States and the United Kingdom, respectively. Harold S. Madsen, of Brigham Young University, reviews the major U.S. proficiency tests, such as the TOEFL, MELAB, and CELT, and specialized tests for such purposes as measuring spoken English proficiency and writing proficiency.

Madsen offers not only a description of each of the tests but also an evaluation, summarizing strengths and weaknesses. J. Charles Alderson, of the University of Lancaster, provides an informative discussion of tests of English proficiency in the United Kingdom, such as the British Council ELTS and the Cambridge Certificate of Proficiency in English. He makes clear some of the differences in testing practice between the United States and the United Kingdom and establishes a basis for interpreting British test reports in the U.S. context.

Chapters Six and Seven deal with two specific areas of English language testing that are receiving increasing attention: the testing of writing skills and the testing of the speaking skills of international teaching assistants. Jane Hughey, of Texas A&M University, discusses ESL composition testing, including the setting of standards and issues involved in establishing a writing evaluation program. She presents a detailed description of existing tests of ESL writing, such as the MELAB Composition and the TOEFL Test of Written English.

Hughey also includes results from a survey of on-campus writing programs and presents examples of procedures and practices actually in use around the country. The problems of evaluating the English language skills of international teaching assistants are discussed in Chapter Seven by Barbara S. Plakans and Roberta G. Abraham, of Iowa State University. They review tests used to assess speaking proficiency, including their advantages and disadvantages, and give practical advice on the establishment of an international teaching assistant (ITA) evaluation program.

In the concluding chapter of the book, Grant Henning, of Educational Testing Service, presents a discussion of the meaning of language test scores from the point of view of a testing professional, but written for the non-specialist test user. He focuses on issues of test validity—what the test tests—and test reliability—how accurately it does so. This chapter is particularly valuable for helping the reader understand why test developers do some of the seemingly strange things they do. Henning also provides concrete advice for the interpretation of test results in light of the many factors that influence the outcome.

This book, then, brings together a wide range of experience and expertise, with a practical orientation. It is hoped that readers will find it both informative and useful in the "real world" of informed decision-making regarding international students in U.S. colleges and universities.

1
Overview of ESL Testing
Ralph Pat Barrett

English language testing has assumed a basic role in the academic life of the international student who wishes to attend an American college or university. Most American institutions today require that all foreign applicants send English test scores along with their admission materials. Scores on the Test of English as a Foreign Language (TOEFL) are almost universally accepted, but some schools also accept scores on the Michigan English Language Assessment Battery (MELAB), the English Proficiency Test of the American Language Institute, Georgetown University (ALI/GU EPT), the Michigan Test of English Language Proficiency (MTELP), and the Comprehensive English Language Test (CELT). Chapter Four contains a full discussion of these tests. However, the screening test used to fulfill the school's English language requirement may only be the beginning of a more extensive testing process. Upon their arrival on campus, international students may be asked to submit to further testing by the school or, in the case of graduate students, by individual academic departments. Such testing may be administered by an intensive English program, by a school testing center, or by the Departments of English, Foreign Languages, English as a Second Language, Linguistics, or Speech. (The term "intensive" refers to programs that engage students in at least 18 hours of English language instruction per week.) Often, this on-campus test will focus on academic skills such as writing, reading, and listening; less often, pronunciation and speaking fluency are included, since not all productive skills are tested on the TOEFL, and many institutions prefer to test academic language skills in the local context.

Even after obtaining the required level on the TOEFL and the on-campus ESL test, some students may have yet another test awaiting them. If they wish to take a position as a teaching assistant on campus, they will probably be required to pass a test of oral English communication. On this test they will be asked to demonstrate their ability to use English effectively in an American classroom situation.

Types of Tests and Their Strengths and Weaknesses

A discussion of English language testing at the college and university level covers a broad range of topics, foremost among them being the types of tests. Educators have become somewhat familiar with the terms that reflect the uses of ESL tests, terms such as *proficiency* (the extent to which a language skill, such as speaking, listening, reading, or writing, has been mastered) and *achievement* (the extent to which specific course material has been mastered). The purpose of the language test calls for other familiar terms: *screening test* (to determine whether the student's English is good enough for him/her to enter full-time study), *placement test* (to determine at which level of ESL study the student should be placed), *diagnostic test* (to determine the relative strengths and weaknesses in the student's English), and *progress test* (to determine how much progress the student has made since the last test).

Another test category involves a dichotomy based on the degree of field testing (trial testing followed by statistical analysis and revision) to which a test has been subjected and the size of the population taking the preliminary version of the test. *Standardized tests* and *teacher-made* or *classroom tests* are distinguished on this basis. Other testing topics of interest concern *what is tested* (the skill area, such as writing, grammar, or listening), the *content area* of the test (such as culture, history, economics, or science), and the *type of scoring* used (subjective or objective).

For some years now, objectively scored language tests (such as the TOEFL) have been favored in situations where large numbers of students are tested at one time. Although time-consuming to prepare, such tests are "reliable" and easy to score. *Reliability* is a concept in testing that refers to the accuracy of the measurement, or how well the test measures whatever it is supposed to measure. Multiple-choice, objective tests have been shown to be very reliable. Many have criticized them, however, voicing doubts about the "validity" of a series of short, unrelated items such as those found on most objective grammar and vocabulary tests. *Validity* is a concept involving the interpretation of test scores in relation to some purpose, such as assessing a candidate's proficiency in English for academic study. Testers using objective tests say that although such items test recognition rather than real language production, the strong relationship between recognition and production warrants their use. Furthermore, performance on objective tests such as the TOEFL has been shown to be related to subsequent academic performance, another argument in favor of their use. (See Chapter Eight for a discussion of reliability and validity concerns.)

Most tests of language production, such as assessments of speaking and writing, are based on samples of actual performance. They often have greater *face validity* (i.e., they "look like" language tests) than objective tests, and are usually far easier to prepare. However, the weakness of tests of language production lies in their lower reliability due to subjective scoring and differences in the production task. The scoring reliability problem can be partly overcome by doing *multiple independent ratings* using two or three highly trained and experienced graders. Using *analytical scoring* (deriving the total score from a set of subscores) rather than holistic scoring (awarding a single score) can also help increase scoring reliability by making the scoring criteria clearer to raters. (Chapter Six contains a discussion of analytical and holistic scoring of writing tests.)

A lack of consistency in the test task that is the basis for evaluation is another source of low reliability in language production tests. For example, suppose that in assessing the speaking ability of two students, one student is asked to give a short talk about an interesting member of his family and the other to talk about her solution to the problem of the balance of payments as it will affect her country in the next ten years. Although it is unlikely that any trained tester would knowingly permit such an outrageous discrepancy among topics, the reliability problem can arise even under the most careful testing conditions. In courses offering *English for Specific Purposes* (ESP), certain writing or speaking topics may unintentionally favor students whose personal background renders the topic easier for them to handle well. For example, in an ESP class for pharmacists, a writing topic dealing with the advantages of generic versus name brand drugs might be more effectively treated by those with some practical experience with generic drugs than by those from countries where these types of drugs are as yet unknown.

Admissions and ESL Testing

In addition to such American screening tests as the TOEFL, the MELAB, and the ALI/GU EPT, several British standardized tests are becoming more widely known. Among these are the English Language Testing Service (ELTS) examination, sponsored by the British Council and the University of Cambridge Local Examinations Syndicate; the Certificate of Proficiency in English as a Foreign Language examination, sponsored by the University of Cambridge Local Examinations Syndicate; and the Communicative Use of English as a Foreign Language test from the Royal Society of Arts Examinations Board. These testing programs are discussed in Chapter Five.

Typically, when a school admissions office receives an English proficiency test score (such as a TOEFL score) from an international applicant, a judgment is quickly made as to whether the applicant's score meets the school's predetermined English requirement (ranging on the TOEFL, for example, from 500 to 550 or 600; on the MELAB, the combined score range may be from 75 to 85). Assuming the applicant has met the school's academic admission requirements, admission will be granted for full-time academic study. But if the score is below the school standard, the applicant may be required to engage in further ESL study. If the school has its own ESL program, or has a cooperative arrangement with an independent program, applicants with weak English test scores may be given a provisional acceptance stipulating that they will be admitted to full-time academic study only when they can meet the school's requirement after some period of language study.

On-Campus Testing

When a prospective international student is referred to a remedial ESL program, almost always the first order of business is another standardized English proficiency test. This initial on-campus test may consist merely of a test of the student's written expression, usually a thirty-minute to one-hour composition on an assigned topic. Typically, this writing test is graded by two or three trained ESL staff members, guided by some sort of agreed-upon scoring criteria and working independently to provide for maximum scoring reliability. In addition to writing, however, many programs require objectively scored subtests of English grammar, vocabulary, reading, and, sometimes, listening. Often, the objective subtests will consist of standardized commercial tests, such as the MTELP or the CELT. Some programs have developed and standardized their own test battery, which may more adequately meet their particular needs. (Chapter Three contains a discussion of on-campus testing.)

The results of the initial on-campus test battery are used in several ways. First, they are used for screening students who were admitted provisionally or were admitted for English study only. On rare occasions, a provisionally admitted student will get a very high "passing" score on the initial test. This may suggest that the student is in fact proficient enough to meet the school's English requirement, but for some reason failed to demonstrate this proficiency on the TOEFL. In such cases, the student may be allowed to begin full-time study on condition that he or she retake the TOEFL at the next opportunity. Equally rare are those cases of passing scores being received by students admitted for English only. It may be possible to arrange immediate admission for such students in an academic program offered by the parent or associated institution.

The next important function of the on-campus ESL test is its most obvious one: to place students in classes at the appropriate level of English language study. One of the characteristics of a typical program is a multilevel structure, usually with classes at elementary, intermediate, and advanced proficiency levels. In addition, the initial test may provide another useful function: that of yielding diagnostic subscores on the separate language skills (listening, speaking, reading, and writing) and language components (grammar and vocabulary). Such diagnostic scores often help ESL instructors to learn more about the students' needs in their classes. In some programs, teachers of a specific skill, such as reading, can examine the results of each student's subtest in that skill to determine individual strengths and weaknesses.

In many ESL programs, students completing a term of study (usually from eight to fifteen weeks in length) are required to take a *parallel form* of the initial on-campus proficiency test. The parallel test, although it appears different in wording, is designed to cover the same content areas and have the same difficulty range as the initial test. The results of the end-of-term test (often called the final examination) are used to determine each student's individual progress as compared with his/her initial scores. As a result, provisionally admitted students who meet the English requirement are permitted to enter full-time academic study in the parent or associated institution, while those with less adequate scores may only be allowed to enroll for part-time academic work. Others, still less qualified, will be enrolled for another term in ESL classes at the same or a higher level.

In some programs, students' progress at term's end is assessed not by means of a parallel test but by nonstandardized *classroom achievement tests* designed by the individual members of the instructional staff. A separate English evaluation is provided for each of the student's classes, the composite of which gives a good picture of the student's relative abilities in English. Other factors, such as the student's study habits, attendance record, motivation, and attitude, might also be reported. The composite evaluation each student receives determines whether the student will be required to re-enroll in ESL classes for another term of study or will be allowed to enroll in the parent or associated school for part-time or full-time academic study.

ESL Testing and Academic Advising

When international students are admitted for full- or part-time academic study, their ESL test scores are usually sent to their academic advisers. Advisers may use this information to tailor an academic program commensurate with the student's strengths and weaknesses in English. For example, they may attempt to place the student with relatively weak listening skills in mathematics classes or other courses where the student may not be subjected to extended lectures. Likewise, those students with weaker reading skills are kept out of courses with heavy schedules of assigned reading, and students having writing difficulties are not enrolled in classes with research paper assignments.

Tests of Oral English Ability. Recently, many U.S. colleges and universities have begun to require additional on-campus proficiency testing of those international graduate students who will have some type of close professional contact with Americans. The largest group of such students are those who are applying for teaching assistantships. Because of widespread complaints by American students that some international teaching assistants have been difficult for them to understand, various screening and placement tests of spoken English performance have been instituted in schools across the United States. The most widely used tests at present appear to be the Test of Spoken English (TSE), produced by Educational Testing Service, and the campus-administered Speaking Proficiency

English Assessment Kit test (SPEAK), the commercial form of the TSE. Other types of tests include oral interviews, oral performance (or communicative competence) tests, and teaching simulations. Often, the content of oral performance tests and teaching simulations is appropriate to the individual student's academic area. For example, a graduate student applying for a teaching assistantship in physics could be required to pronounce a set of terms commonly used in physics, explain an article from a physics journal or text, and/or demonstrate the teaching of a concept or principle from physics.

The scoring of such production tests is subjective and requires highly trained raters to evaluate the quality of the student's communicative ability, cultural awareness, and pedagogic skills. Some areas for assessment include the student's spoken English (pronunciation, grammar, vocabulary, fluency, etc.), listening comprehension (handling of questions, understanding of instructions, etc.), and communication strategies (requesting repetition of unclear questions, paraphrasing answers, using hesitation markers such as "umm," "ah," and "OK"). Other areas evaluated are the student's familiarity with the subculture of the U.S. classroom (appropriate use of names, proper acknowledgement of correct answers, appropriate use of correction techniques, etc.) and teaching skills (organization of material, ability to present new concepts, use of the chalkboard, use of eye contact, etc.). The testing of international teaching assistants is discussed in detail in Chapter Seven.

Other international groups that have recently been asked to undergo oral performance testing are medical science students and visiting scholars and researchers. In the case of medical and nursing students, adequate communicative skills are felt to be necessary since an important part of their training may include frequent close contact with American patients. Visiting scholars and researchers sometimes present lectures in academic courses, and although not technically students, occasionally attend classes as well. In any case, they usually must be able to communicate with their American colleagues in order to successfully accomplish their mission in the United States.

Test Administration and Facilities. In addition to quiet, well-lighted rooms suitable for large test administration, facilities for testing might include a language laboratory in which to do large-group listening or speaking tests. However, as more and more schools establish computer and video laboratories, more testing will likely be done using these technological tools. For example, it has been shown that testing time can be significantly shortened through the use of *interactive adaptive testing* on the computer. In such tests, the students begin the test with material of intermediate difficulty, and, depending on the accuracy of their responses, are branched either to easier or more difficult items. In this way, the students do not waste time dealing with inappropriate test material. It is likely that the use of the interactive videodisc for video-based adaptive testing will also become popular when and if its cost decreases. (At present, interactive video costs several thousand dollars per unit.) Also costly at present is speech analysis computer software, but such products as Visi-Pitch (Kay Elemetrics Company) and Speech Spectrographic Display 8800 (Kay Elemetrics Company) can be adapted for use in the testing of English articulation and stress.

Testing English for Specific Purposes. Whoever said that form follows function was not referring to English language testing, but the expression nevertheless seems quite appropriate. The function of the English language program serves to determine the form and content of the ESL tests that are administered to its students. In programs whose main function it is to prepare international students for academic study, the content of the English test is heavily influenced by those language skills that students must have to succeed in school. Most often these skills include the writing style of research papers and reports, the listening comprehension ability to understand college lectures, and the reading skills to handle college textbook material.

In ESL programs whose primary function is to prepare foreign immigrants and refugees for life in the United States, the testing is biased toward "survival" English, the comprehension of idiomatic conversational English, the writing of job applications, business letters, and official forms, and the reading of newspapers, notices, menus, and time schedules. Likewise, in programs that have large groups of students specializing in physics, chemistry, engineering, economics, agriculture, education, or some other specific academic area, the content of the ESL testing program usually reflects the students' academic field.

The Future of ESL Testing

What does the future hold for ESL testing in U.S. colleges and universities? Test content will likely be more and more related to the specific subject areas that international students are studying. For example, tests can be based on the kinds of reading, writing, and listening tasks that students face in chemistry, math, or physics classes. We may also see further integration of language and culture in testing, particularly if classes for international teaching assistants continue to focus on the American classroom culture as a part of English language training. Likewise, as ESL teachers continue to stress communicative competence (the ability to communicate in a linguistically and culturally acceptable manner), we will see tests becoming more subjective in nature and more focused on the students' *ability to do something,* rather than merely on their *knowledge of how to do it.* This, in turn, will call for improved methods of training raters to conduct and score subjective evaluations. It will certainly call for the use of technological tools such as the computer and the videodisc, not only to make economical use of the time allotted for testing but also to present realistic language situations for testing by means of graphic simulations and videotape.

Conclusion

In theory, the perfect English language test for the international student would be easy to devise: if we could somehow put each student into a great variety of absolutely authentic situations in which English must be used to succeed, we could award the student a score commensurate with the degree of success attained. Unfortunately, we have neither the time, the personnel, nor the facilities to realize such a fantasy. The best we can do is to continue to make our ESL testing as valid, as reliable, and as practical as possible with the limited resources we have. Considering their importance to the future of our world, our international students deserve no less.

2
English Language Testing: The View from the Admissions Office
G. James Haas

This chapter will focus on the duties of college admissions officers with regard to the preliminary assessment of their international students' general English skills at the time of application. It discusses how these officials might share their insights with their campus constituencies, and what their role is in seeing that the decision of the campus concerning an applicant's English language skills is properly conveyed to the applicant in the admissions process.

Before an admissions officer can productively execute these functions, the institution needs to have made some fundamental decisions about the level of English skills it can accommodate among its international student population. For example, will the institution offer an intensive English program? Will it offer only supplemental English courses? Will it accept only those students capable of full-time academic work upon arrival? Or will it choose some combination of these options?

The various segments of an institution may differ in their approaches to this issue. An academic department with far too many applicants might set a high standard for admission as a kinder alternative to encouraging the linguistically lesser qualified to spend the time and money involved in completing an application. Reducing application paperwork can also benefit the reviewing institution economically.

Decisions such as these need to be made in consultation with a wide representation of those people on campus most concerned with international admissions, ESL evaluation and teaching, freshman composition, and subject-area teaching. In particular, admissions officers need to rely on the expertise of ESL professionals, on campus and in the field, in making policy decisions about the level of English language proficiency the institution can accept, the need for on-campus testing, and the need for intensive and/or supplemental ESL courses.

An institution should carefully consider how aspects of these choices might be implemented. It may be able to pool resources with neighboring institutions to create an intensive English program or offer supplemental English courses. Alternatively, an institution might offer conditional academic admission, with the applicant agreeing to come to the United States for intensive English training prior to beginning academic work. An agreed-upon time frame and/or level of achievement can be designated in such arrangements, as can the specific intensive English program to be attended.

Setting Institutional English Language Admission Standards

The following observations assume that an institution does not have an "open admissions" policy with regard to the English skills of its applicants (i.e., that the institution plans to establish standards by which it will admit only students capable of undertaking some academic work upon arrival).

The nature and levels of the institution's programs will help determine whether there should be a single institutional standard of English proficiency, or whether requirements might be vary by department and program. For example, an institution with a number of technical, terminal programs may be able to work with lower levels of English proficiency than one with only academic tracks. ESL professionals, other faculty members, and administrators would need to be involved in setting the English standards to be required. Before such institutional standards are set and referenced to some standardized test score, the terminology to be used in the discussions should be clarified. To that end, members of the policy setting committee should obtain advice from professional bodies such as NAFSA, the University Consortium of Intensive English Programs (UCIEP), and Teachers of English to Speakers of Other Languages (TESOL). Such groups can provide descriptive and practical information about proficiency levels from basic to advanced, the language skills (reading, writing, speaking, and listening) required in different disciplines, and the type of program needed for students at each level.

The next step is to determine how standardized test scores relate to the various levels of proficiency expected (i.e., what scores the institution will require at each level of proficiency). Such decisions should not be made in isolation from the realities of individual schools; at this stage, a flexible approach to the development of guidelines for evaluating English skills is best. In this way, the committee can make adjustments from time to time, based on discussions with ESL professionals.

On-Campus Retesting

After assessing preliminary reports, institutions should generally retest newly arrived foreign students who come from countries where English is not the first language. For the sake of fairness and administrative sanity, it may be best to retest everyone who falls under this guideline, however plausible the grounds for exception. Retesting should not cause hardship to students if the tests are administered without charge and the results are provided with a one- or two-day turnaround.

There are several reasons why a retesting program is highly advisable as part of the admissions and registration process. Retesting will reveal such extremes as applicants with scores of 600 or more on the Test of English as a Foreign Language (TOEFL) who need supplemental English courses, applicants with scores in the low 500s who need no further English courses, and those at or near the 500 level who need full-time intensive English. In many such cases, the TOEFL has been taken under proper conditions and without special coaching on the intricacies of "beating" standardized tests. The factors in favor of doing on-campus retesting may be summarized as follows:

1. *Time lag.* Language skills are not static; they can change considerably over a 12-month period. Most preliminary test reports will be several months old by the time the student arrives to register.
2. *Inconsistency.* The institution needs to know if there are significant discrepancies between applicants' preliminary English assessments and their skills as revealed upon arrival.
3. *Coaching.* There are TOEFL-teaching (as opposed to English-teaching) schools that claim to make a student more "test smart." Students from these schools may achieve higher test scores than their actual English language skills warrant, although coaching of this type will not increase test scores significantly.
4. *Forgery.* Very occasionally, an individual will manage to provide an entirely falsified report.

The retesting program may be as extensive or brief as the institution feels is necessary, and has the resources for. An important component of any retest should be a one- or two-page composition on a non-threatening topic. Institutions may wish to supplement the writing sample with an institutional TOEFL, the Michigan Test, or their own diagnostic test, if one is already in place. They may wish, too, to assess speaking proficiency by means of an oral interview. More will be said about these issues in the chapters on on-campus placement testing, the testing of writing, and the evaluation of international teaching assistants.

What procedures should be followed in cases where a student fails a retest, and the institution in question has no ESL program? As a routine part of their admission information, all students should be forewarned of the possibility that their English language skills, if found deficient, may prevent them from enrollment. It is legal, according to INS regulations, to refer the student to an ESL program elsewhere. Assuming an F-1 student visa had been granted, the second institution would simply need to issue a new I-20 to the student. The first institution could postpone the start of the academic program until the student's English had been sufficiently strengthened.

The student who fails the retest will likely be disappointed, to say the least. However, the institution should, from the beginning, make clear its policy on retesting and the consequences of not passing the test. The only alternatives such a student has are yet another round of retesting or enrollment in the recommended language program. Making exceptions does not benefit either the student or the institution in the long run, and sets up a precedent. Once an exception is made, others will hear of it and request similar treatment. Students who fail English screening will sometimes plead for an exception on the basis of their financial situation. However, standards of English, once established, should be considered nonnegotiable. To waive them because an individual claims financial problems is to compromise the institution's professional credibility.

Some Unreliable Preliminary Reports

From time to time, students offer English language proficiency reports whose reliability might be considered questionable. While the admissions officer might provisionally accept such evidence under certain circumstances, students allowed to proceed on the basis of such reports need to be forewarned that institutional retesting will finally determine when they can start their academic program. Among unreliable preliminary indicators are the following:

1. Good grades in English awarded to students from non-English-speaking countries. These grades may reflect literary or grammar studies, often with little or no attention to language as it is used in natural communication.
2. A B.A. (or equivalent) in English from a non-English-speaking country. This degree is sometimes awarded to students with weak oral/aural skills who have had infrequent contact with native English speakers.
3. A "satisfactory" verbal score on the Scholastic Aptitude Test (SAT), Graduate Records Examination (GRE), or similar examination. These examinations make no pretense of assessing proficiency in English as a second language and should not be used to do so.
4. Applicants' personal assessment of their skills and good intentions of pursuing further English training prior to their arrival in the United States.
5. One year or less of study in an English-speaking country (including the United States) as part of a special program, or in a situation where the academic load was light and/or in a narrowly defined subject area.
6. The opinion of a faculty member or administrator who has had only casual contact with a prospective student. This is especially the case when the contact was made abroad; under such circumstances, the ability to assess English skills may diminish. Friends or relatives who do much of the talking on behalf of a prospective student can also skew one's perspective.

Admissions officers should rely on the assessments of ESL professionals who are experienced in evaluating the English level of non-native speakers. In any case, it is essential that the student be informed in writing of admissions procedures and of the consequences if an exception is made. The student should also understand the process of verifying English proficiency after arrival on campus.

Interpreting Preliminary English Reports

Too often those who receive English reports, which are predominantly in the form of standardized test scores, do not appreciate these items for what they are: preliminary assessments administered at a given time and place. They are not irrevocable assessments of English proficiency, nor are they in themselves guarantees of academic success, no matter how high the scores. Rather, they are one of the many factors to be considered in the overall admissions process.

Certainly, it is not only U.S. institutions who misuse test reports. U.S. and foreign government officials, foundations, and other agencies all contribute to the myth that some absolute score guarantees English proficiency. The story is even told of a man who required a certain TOEFL score of his daughter's suitor before the marriage could take place! It is small wonder that international applicants frequently write to say that they have already met the English requirement for study in the United States. Whose standard they have managed to meet is usually not stated.

TOEFL Reports. Since the TOEFL is the predominant testing instrument in use today, we should familiarize ourselves with TOEFL reports and how they might be used. The following observations are based on experiences at Indiana University, which over the past decade has enrolled some 2,000 international students on its main campus each academic year. These students represent over 100 countries.

Experience at Indiana shows that the majority of students whose TOEFL scores are 600 and above will likely be able to enroll in a regular full-time graduate or undergraduate program; those scoring in the 560 to 590 range will be able to handle a minimum full-time load of academic work; those in the 500 to 550 range should have a program of half-time academic work and half-time supplemental English; those in the 460 to 490 range may be able to handle one academic course if the rest of their program is in supplemental English; and those in the low 400s or below are in need of full-time intensive English. These broad-stroke expectations have been corroborated by retesting in 75 to 80 percent of the cases.

Institutions with graduate programs are especially likely to have a variety of English standards. For instance, they may have a range of standards for admission-only situations and a separate standard for applicants who are to be considered for teaching assistantships. In light of recent lawsuits across the country and legislation in some states concerning the English skills of international teaching assistants, it is important that a preliminary English report on such an applicant indicate strong promise, and it is essential that the accepting institution retest before placing the student in a teaching situation. The issue of the English language testing of international teaching assistants is discussed in detail in Chapter Seven.

Teaching assistants aside, let us assume that an institution has general guidelines for both graduates and undergraduates on the meaning of certain TOEFL scores, as suggested above. Considering the total score alone can be likened to diagnosing an illness by taking only the patient's temperature; the risk of being incorrect is greatly increased. In interpreting the overall TOEFL score, make use of the three subscores: Listening Comprehension, Structure and Written Expression, and Vocabulary and Reading Comprehension. While the two-digit figures reported for these subtests may at first seem hard to interpret, adding a zero will indicate how each score would look as an overall TOEFL score (e.g., 46 = 460; 62 = 620). While not recommended by Educational Testing Service, this "rule-of-thumb" procedure will allow admissions officers and departmental admissions committees to judge the abilities of applicants in the three broad areas of listening, writing, and reading skills, and indicate where extra help might be required.

Clearly, the idea of an absolute cut-off score for the TOEFL is ill-conceived. Testing devices are too inaccurate to support such fine discrimination. However, admission decisions still have to be made. Therefore, if an institution's research and experience with retesting suggest that a 550 level of proficiency is indicative of minimum needs, the admissions officer might consider admission of a candidate with a 10-17 point deficient score. (The Standard Error of Measurement [SEM] on the TOEFL total score is 14.1 [ETS 1987, 26], hence the suggestion of the 10-17 point range as a margin for error, since TOEFL total scores can only end in 0, 3, or 7.) The offer of admission on this basis may be conditional, or something other than full admission. If an institution is prepared to consider alternatives, an offer of summer English before the academic year is better than a denial. If, on the other hand, an institution firmly believes that a 550 score reflects an absolute minimum level of English, then that institution's materials should speak of a 560 or 570 general requirement, with some behind-the-scenes allowance for students with scores of 10 to 20 points lower than the stated minimum. International applicants will find this approach fairer than the 550/547, yes/no approach; moreover, making allowance for the SEM is less frustrating for all concerned because a small miss is harder for the student to accept and more difficult for the institution to justify.

Other U.S. Standardized Tests. Once an institution and its departments have developed experience with TOEFL scores, they often become reluctant to accept other evidence of English ability. However, if an institution is interested in advancing its international activities, it will need to show some flexibility in procedures when it is impractical or impossible for a particular student to sit for the TOEFL. This does not mean that the institution must compromise its standards; rather, scores from other standardized tests should be accepted as evidence of proficiency in English. Two such examinations are the American Language Institute, Georgetown University English Proficiency Test (ALI/GU EPT) and the Michigan English Language Assessment Battery (MELAB).

ALI/GU EPT scores usually accompany an application that is connected with a U.S. government agency such as the U.S. Agency for International Development or the U.S. Information Agency. The ALI/GU EPT is a new test that has replaced the old ALI/GU, which many test users are more familiar with. The old ALI/GU is now viewed by the ALI as retired and its security is suspect. More information on its replacement can be found in Chapter Four.

The MELAB is given in some 120 countries. The English Language Institute at Michigan reports scores on a 0-100 scale and provides interpretive information. Small studies have been conducted in which applicants took the MELAB and the TOEFL within a reasonably close time frame (see, for example, the TOEFL Test and Score Manual 1987, 28), and it has been found that the two tests are substantially correlated, that is, they appear to be testing many of the same abilities. One can devise a way to compare MELAB and TOEFL results, at least within a key range of scores (70 to 90 percent). The formula is as follows: MELAB score x 6 + 20 = TOEFL.

Thus, a MELAB score of 80 is multiplied by six, which equals 480; add 20 and the result of 500 can be interpreted as roughly equivalent to a 500-level TOEFL achievement. Those scoring below a 70 on the MELAB are very likely to need intensive English before entering regular academic courses. Those scoring above 90 may well achieve 600-level TOEFL scores.

This procedure is not recommended by ETS or the Michigan English Language Institute and should be regarded as only a very rough estimate of comparability. One has to assume in making these comparisons that the test taker had not been attempting practice versions of the same test repeatedly before taking the final one. One should also be certain that the applicants took a secure version of the test in question. (See the discussion of MELAB and ALI/GU in Chapter Four.)

The above formula is certainly not a high precision instrument; however, it can produce useful estimates for the admissions officer who must make admission decisions based on a TOEFL criterion but without a TOEFL score from individual students.

Reports from Non-U.S. Tests. English reports sent from the People's Republic of

China in the recent past have shown information from the English Proficiency Test or Visiting Scholars Test. These were on a scale of 0-160. A score of 105 seems roughly akin to 500 on the TOEFL. On the basis of 105, a score of 15 points either way is comparable to 50 points on the TOEFL; i.e., 90 = 450, 120 = 550, etc. As the TOEFL and MELAB gain acceptance in the People's Republic, the use of these Chinese examinations seems to be on the wane.

Applicants from countries with historical ties to the United Kingdom often submit GCE O-Levels (General Certificate of Education, Ordinary Level). These exams are normally taken at the end of the fifth form (11th grade). A pass in English Language at O-Level with a grade of A, B, or C seems to represent a greater level of overall English ability than would a TOEFL in the upper 550 range. Assuming this O-Level report was produced under the jurisdiction of one of the five or six British-based examination boards, Indiana University will waive its TOEFL requirement for the student in question. (See the discussion of British tests in Chapter Five.)

Certain other British testing instruments can likely be equated to TOEFL scores. Those scoring in Band 7 or higher on the English Language Testing Service (ELTS) test (conducted by the British Council) will be quite ready to undertake full-time study at a U.S. institution. The ELTS is discussed in Chapter Five.

One group of non-native English speakers whose proficiency cannot easily be placed on a TOEFL scale but who nevertheless will likely have strong English skills is that of European university-level English majors. These students usually score above the 550 range on the TOEFL, particularly if they have spent a period of six months or more in English-speaking countries.

Applicants Without Preliminary Reports

A troublesome group of international applicants for many U.S. institutions consists of those who submit no English report at all. Such students explain that their skills are insufficient and that they plan to come to the United States for intensive English training prior to starting their academic work. They seek a conditional admission, contingent upon successful completion of English study in the United States.

Many admissions officers feel uneasy in dealing with this type of applicant because of the uncertainty involved: How fast will the student's English skills progress? In which session will he or she want to join the academic program? What if the student's English program finishes at a time when it is not possible to enroll in academic courses? How do we handle those students who insist that their English skills are ready before their intensive English program agrees? How do we deal with the individual whose aptitude for mastering English is low? There may be many reasons for not wanting to work with such applicants.

In deciding how to proceed with students who seek conditional admission while they concentrate on English language skills, an institution needs to assess carefully its program capabilities, enrollment pressures, and long-range goals in international educational exchange. If the internal bureaucratic procedures are flexible, then some fair questions to ask are: What alternatives does the student have for improving English skills if not admitted? How fast can a student's English be expected to improve? In denying admission, is the institution simply unwilling to take the chance of facing an impatient individual who wants to enter academic work before his or her English skills are ready? If such questions can be resolved, and if the institution has a retesting program in place and faith in the skills of its ESL personnel, it is worth the effort to work with students who need significant English improvement prior to attempting academic work. Ideally, the institution should have its own intensive English program or be familiar enough with other intensive English programs in the United States that its admissions personnel feel secure in the training and evaluation reports that the latter provide.

Another group of international applicants that may require special consideration are those from countries where English is the official language, such as Australia, the Bahamas, Barbados, New Zealand, and the United Kingdom. These students should be exempt from U.S. preliminary English testing requirements. If citizens of these countries are lacking in English language skills, their deficiencies will be similar to those found in graduates of regular U.S. high schools. The TOEFL and similar testing instruments are not the proper diagnostic tests for this group. Canada should be considered an English-speaking country, with the exception of Quebec, which is primarily a French-speaking province. Countries of the Indian sub-continent would usually not fall into the English-as-the-official-language category, since English is only one official language, and many applicants will not have used it in the home. Applicants from India, Bangladesh, and Pakistan should, therefore, be treated in the same way as those from other, non-English-speaking countries and be required to show evidence of proficiency in English.

The Admissions Process

The international admissions process should be centralized in order to simplify the assessment of English reports. Institutions should also learn to review these reports in the context of the total application file and not in isolation. Knowing from preliminary reports the general level of an applicant's English gives an admissions officer some indication of a likely date for that student to begin regular classes following additional English training (if needed).

It is extremely important in the admissions process to convey complete, accurate information to the applicants to avoid surprises about an institution's policies, the preliminary English language assessment procedures, and retesting. The latter should also be described briefly in letters of admission. For those who show weaker preliminary English reports, an additional line should be added to the letter of admission, for example, "The results of your May 1988 (name of test) report suggest that you may/will need to spend at least part of your first term in supplemental English courses." Those who have agreed to come to the United States for intensive English training before they begin academic study also need to be reminded of the commitment and have conditions of admission explained. In such cases, it is best to quote the earliest possible date for starting an academic program, as well as back-up dates in case more English training should be needed. Finally, if an institution charges a new application fee each time a student changes entry dates, this policy should be reassessed to accommodate students who require intensive English training. Not only does it seem unfair to penalize students who are being delayed while they improve these key skills needed for academic success, but it is also not wise recruitment policy.

Summary

Assessing active English skills in the admissions process is generally an imprecise task. Preliminary reports need to be appreciated both for what they are and what they are not. They do represent insights into the English language skills of applicants at a given time in the past, but they may not reflect the skills with which students arrive at an institution. The receiving institution is therefore well-advised to: (a) have a retesting program in place for new arrivals; (b) not use absolute cut-off test scores in the admission process; and (c) consider using ESL programs in the United States as another tool in their admissions process. Institutions interested in enrolling foreign students need to consider ways of avoiding these difficulties by having contingency plans in place. Working with varying levels of English skills is one important facet of the enrollment process.

The English language skills (or lack thereof) of international students are not something to be feared; they simply need to be addressed. No outside source can answer all the questions of a particular institution. Nevertheless, an experienced team of ESL professionals, admissions personnel, international advisers, and subject-area faculty can develop sound policies that are based on the needs and objectives of both the institution and its international student population.

3
English Language Testing: The View from the English Teaching Program
Paul J. Angelis

Given the diversity of U.S. higher education, it should not be surprising to find that no one system of English language proficiency testing and placement is in operation at all campuses. For this reason, it would be impractical to describe the many different testing schemes employed. It is realistic, however, to review the common features of most testing systems along with some general guidelines under which they operate. It is also appropriate to address the issue of who to test, and for what purpose. This will lead to what many would consider the central question: what kinds of tests are used and how are they incorporated into the testing and placement process? A process orientation underlies the entire discussion. If the elements (both human and nonhuman) of the placement process and how they interact with each other are understood, progress will have been made toward understanding the system as a whole.

This chapter focuses on using on-campus testing to make decisions about whether international students require additional instruction in English language skills—and if so, at what level. Thus, this chapter is about placement testing. The options for placement range from (1) no further English language classes (usually in the case of graduate students, or immediate placement into "freshman composition" in the case of undergraduates), to (2) restricting regular courseloads while some classes in ESL are taken, to (3) full-time ESL in an intensive program with no regular coursework.

Issues in Placement Testing

Who should be tested, and what specific objectives are usually set? The most basic and obvious response is, students whose native language is not English. Immediately, however, some distinctions must be made. The issue of native language is not as obvious as it seems. Foreign student status and the need for English language testing are not parallel. While it is usually clear that most students from Canada, Australia, and the United Kingdom should not be subject to English language testing, the situation for students from many other parts of the world—for example, India or Pakistan—is not so obvious. Information collected from the student's application concerning first language(s) learned and used should determine the need for testing.

Of greater concern is the question of how on-campus testing relates to other English language testing for foreign students. Testing conducted on site, prior to the student's beginning academic work, is generally the second occasion on which information is collected about a student's English proficiency, since most institutions require applicants to present evidence of English language proficiency as part of the application process. While some applicants are already in the United States, prospective students applying from overseas are not available for on-site testing. A policy issue immediately arises. At what point is English proficiency determined, and when and how does on-campus testing enter the picture? The first priority should be the applicant's academic qualifications, not English language proficiency.

Three Hypothetical Examples

The same is true for placement testing. All students who are tested on campus should already have met academic requirements for admission. This being the case, how do the application review and the on-site testing relate? At what point is an admissions decision made, and what additional decisions result from testing? Consider three hypothetical situations:

1. At institution A, all English language proficiency decisions are made during the application review. Policies are established for determining levels of proficiency required as well as necessary academic credentials. Applicants are informed either that they are admitted or not. Only those who are admitted are free to come to the institution to begin their studies. Once they arrive, no further testing is done.
2. At institution B, similar procedures are followed in reviewing the status of applicants, except that additional English language testing takes place for some students when they arrive on campus. The choice of which students to test at the time of arrival must be made in advance, and some notification should be provided to applicants in the institution's catalog and promotional brochures. It could be the case, for example, that all graduate applicants are required to take on-campus placement tests, but not undergraduates. Or, a more common situation, applicants above a certain level in English proficiency are exempted from further testing. Those below, but within some specified limit, are not.

3. At institution C, after initial screening based on some predetermined level of English language proficiency, all students who arrive on campus are tested. (If no such first cut is made, of course, all applicants meeting academic requirements would be eligible to come—a highly impractical way to proceed.) Institutions that follow this option usually have intensive English programs available on their campuses, because placement testing works best with multiple options. A typical procedure would call for all students with application scores of 450 or more on the Test of English as a Foreign Language (TOEFL) to be tested on arrival in order to obtain an accurate indication of English proficiency at the time the person is actually beginning studies, and to evaluate students' abilities in speaking or technical writing, which the TOEFL does not test.

For students with lesser proficiency, on-site testing provides an opportunity to determine what deficiencies may be present and what immediate English training may be the most appropriate. It is not wise to enter such a situation with no baseline level of proficiency in mind; thus, there is a need to allow students above a certain minimum level to be tested. Furthermore, the availability of an institution's own intensive English program creates the possibility of placing an applicant in intensive training for as much as a quarter or semester if that is warranted.

Applicants Already in the United States

A substantial number of students apply for admission from intensive English language programs in the United States. It is not uncommon for a college or university to apply the same admissions standards and criteria for these students as for applicants from abroad. Often, however, the situation provides for some differences. Especially when applicants come from an institution's own ESL program or another one nearby, it is possible, and may be preferable, to rely on a combination of test scores and English language assessment data provided by the ESL program to arrive at a clearer picture of an applicant's English proficiency. In this case, admissions and placement testing can be combined.

In a typical situation, the ESL program conducts its end-of-term proficiency testing for students who are nearing the end of English training. A battery of tests is administered that yields a profile of English language proficiency. Frequently, this battery includes a general proficiency test, often standardized and objective, given to all students. Those who score within a certain range would participate in additional testing, usually more direct and often individually based. Writing samples and oral interviews are commonly a part of this second stage. The reason for focusing on a subset of students for a second stage of testing is largely economic: for those who score at the extreme upper end of the scale, further testing may be redundant. Using the TOEFL scale, for example, it may be appropriate to dispense with additional testing for those with scores of

580 to 600 or higher. Likewise, those with scores at the other end of the scale may not yet be at the point where finer-tuned placement testing is necessary. TOEFL scale scores of 400 or less, for example, usually indicate the need for further full-time intensive English training.

Types of Tests

Two important questions need to be considered concerning the use of tests for placement. First is the matter of the tests themselves. What kinds of tests are available and how do they differ? Second is the nature of the system in which placement tests are administered. If such screening of English language skills is to be meaningful, there must be careful consideration of the information required and how testing can provide this information.

Standardized Tests. The simplest option is to select an externally developed test that can be secured for administration when needed. Tests such as the Test of English as a Foreign Language (TOEFL), the Michigan Test of English Language Proficiency (MTELP) and the Comprehensive English Language Test (CELT) have been used extensively for on-site testing. Forms of these tests are available either on a purchase or a loan basis. It is true that they are generally considered proficiency tests rather than placement tests. However, their results can be interpreted for placement purposes. For example, subscores provided for the various parts or sections of the test are particularly useful in providing immediate and current information. Looking at differential performance between listening and reading skills, for instance, can help to guide placement decisions. *Reviews of English Language Proficiency Tests* (Alderson, Krahnke, and Stansfield 1987) provides a comprehensive summary of tests available for English language assessment of non-native speakers.

Regardless of which tests of this type may be selected, the results will, of necessity, be somewhat limited. The information provided (on both content and format) is often neither appropriate nor detailed enough to resolve placement issues. An alternative is to develop a test strictly for use in a given college or university situation. However, designing such an instrument is no easy task. A good standardized test requires experienced personnel, time, and funds for development and trial testing. Even success in such an endeavor will yield a single test that will require regular updating and evaluation as well as the continued development of alternative editions. Thus, this option is often impractical.

Speaking and Writing Tests. More elaborate testing schemes are those that combine a standardized test with other measures—usually those that rely on more direct techniques—to give placement information. The mechanisms used are similar to those in the combined proficiency/placement programs described above. A variety of approaches can be used to determine whether all or some students are to be tested and, if some, which ones. The two most common types of tests used to provide information on how best to "place" non-native speakers of English are those that focus on speaking and writing tasks.

Speaking Tests. Speaking tests are those that attempt to determine how well new students are able to use their ability in oral English to perform certain tasks. A few ready-made tests are available for on-campus testing. For the most part, these are tests that require the student to record his or her responses to questions put forward in oral, written, or visual form. The most common format for doing so is the audio tape, which is then available for scoring, as with the TSE/SPEAK test (Educational Testing Service 1983). Oral tests that employ an actual interview and are administered and/or scored by both ESL personnel and subject specialists from departments where the students are enrolled are the most comprehensive and appear to have the most solid foundation in terms of content and procedure. Both tape-recorded and live interview tests require that trained personnel at the college or university administer and rate students' performance. Because of the time required to administer such tests, it is rare that all new non-native speakers will be tested. Instead, the test may be required for those with a particular need for oral skills: graduate students, and especially, graduate students who are being considered for teaching assistantships. This category of students has come under careful scrutiny because of the sensitive nature of their position within higher education. Many testing schemes have been instituted for this situation, and the choice of which tests to use and when to administer them is linked closely to the policies an institution has set. Some universities try to assign graduate teaching assistantships when students first arrive. In this case, the institution may rely on information available during the admissions review, including results from tests such as the Test of Spoken English. For universities that consider candidates for teaching assistantships only after one or two years of study, there will usually be no such testing until that point. Under these circumstances, there is less reason to consider it placement testing, but rather, a special type of screening for a specific purpose. The issues in the testing of speaking proficiency for ITAs are discussed in detail in Chapter Seven.

Writing Tests. Like oral ability, writing is a skill that has been the focus of placement testing. Once again, its relevance to an individual's academic performance is clear. For both graduate students and undergraduates, the academic requirements imposed in most fields entail writing ability, whether in thesis preparation or freshman composition. Two types of tests have been increasingly relied upon for this purpose: holistic and analytical. In both cases, actual writing samples are collected. That is, students are asked to write brief compositions or essays on assigned topics. What differs is the rating system used.

The first system is a completely holistic one. No detailed analyses are made of the student's writing. Rather, an overall rating is assigned, which serves to categorize the writing according to predetermined criteria. The establishment of such categories, typically using a rating scale, can be a means of determining a student's readiness for academic writing, signal weaknesses, and point toward the need for further preparatory work in writing.

The second system usually also yields an overall holistic rating, but provides, in addition, numerical and verbal indicators of how well the writer has mastered many of the subcomponents of writing (e.g., grammar, vocabulary, and organization). For those students who may be weak writers, this latter system provides helpful diagnostic as well as placement information; the profile of the student's writing can help to decide how much additional work in writing the student may need and what particular subskills may be lacking.

In either case, a direct placement test of writing requires careful preparation, thorough training of raters, and the identification of appropriate criteria. Regular updating of information is required to ensure that criteria and ratings are consistent and appropriate for the objectives of the screening and placement process. Chapter Eight contains a detailed discussion of the issues in the testing of writing ability.

The Placement Process

Regardless of the tests used or of the procedures for selecting, screening, and placing students, certain guidelines apply to the process as a whole. If placement is to be done properly, a college or university must take full advantage of the resources it has available, tailor the testing to the programs and setting at hand, and link the testing to training options available. The personnel required include two major groups: those who are knowledgeable about the language skills being measured and those with expertise in testing and measurement. In some instances, an individual or group with dual expertise is in charge of placement testing; this person or group determines options for testing, sets up the system, and monitors it throughout.

If placement testing is to be meaningful, it should also take full advantage of informed knowledge about students' needs. This means having good information about the English language demands on students at different levels and in different departments. In a comprehensive university, it should be possible to establish differences in English language requirements, for example, among graduate students in the physical sciences, undergraduates in business, and teaching assistants in engineering. Relevant information should be gathered by consulting faculty members in the appropriate fields, current and former students, and English language training personnel. Such data are often difficult to collect and are subject to change over time, but they help to clarify students' needs and abilities. For example, if information suggests graduate students in the university's MBA program must rely on their spoken English skills for making individual and group presentations, then oral placement testing could be necessary.

An associated element in the placement testing process is the availability of options for placement itself, that is, of courses or training programs in English language skills. The most elaborate testing system, even if based on a thorough analysis of needs, is incomplete if not accompanied by the final element: a battery of well-developed courses in ESL for students who lack certain skills.

General Guidelines

No matter what type of placement system a college or university may adopt, and regardless of the overall system in which it operates, certain basic principles should be followed. Many of the issues involved have already been cited. Five guidelines are critical:

1. Clearly establish goals and policies. Why is placement testing needed? Who is to be tested? What are the projected outcomes of the testing?
2. Seek out and involve all personnel with the expertise required for testing of this type. Key persons are those with training and experience in ESL and in testing and measurement. Early decisions will relate to choices for selecting, adapting, or developing tests, and ensuring that appropriately trained personnel are available in sufficient numbers to support the program chosen.
3. Establish close links with all units involved with foreign student admissions and matriculation. While placement testing is different from, and separate from, admissions testing, it must be closely coordinated within the institution's overall system and administered by an admissions office, graduate school, or individual departments. Since placement testing takes place when students arrive, it needs to be coordinated with other placement and orientation activities usually conducted by an international programs office.
4. Carefully tie placement testing to whatever combination of training programs or courses are available for those students who need additional training in English. Courses should be available in a number of skill areas and for specialized needs. Those units and personnel involved in offering such courses should be involved in, or at least kept abreast of, the types of placement tests given.
5. Regularly evaluate the placement testing system to determine its effectiveness. Does feedback from subsequent review of student performance confirm the results of testing? Are those recommended for no further training still deficient in any significant areas? How appropriate has subsequent training been for those placed as a result of testing?

Placement testing programs may differ widely from place to place, and legitimately so. In fact, placement testing is not even necessary in every instance. However, awareness of the issues discussed above should help to determine whether such testing is needed, and what should be considered in planning and implementing such a program.

4
Standardized ESL Tests Used in U.S. Colleges and Universities
Harold S. Madsen

The standardized ESL tests most frequently associated with American colleges and universities are those used in the admissions process. While some U.S. colleges and universities accept overseas English as a second or foreign language (ESL or EFL) test scores, most institutions are oriented towards scores from tests produced in the United States. Therefore this discussion will be restricted to commercial U.S. tests used for college admission. Chapter Five can be consulted for information on British academic EFL tests at upper school levels.

ESL Tests Used for General Admission

The TOEFL. The Test of English as a Foreign Language (TOEFL) is used for college or university admission in the United States more than all other commercial exams combined (British or American). Administered worldwide 12 times annually, the TOEFL is taken by approximately 510,000 students each academic year—most seeking admission to American institutions of higher learning.

Description. The TOEFL is an all-objective, three-section exam that tests listening comprehension, reading comprehension (as well as vocabulary mastery), and competence in recognizing appropriate written expression. Instructions and examples are in English. No question on any of the 12 administrations is ever used on a subsequent administration. Actual examination time is 105 minutes, with separate time limits on each of the three sections. The TOEFL is not for sale; candidates, who pay a fee to take the test, must register in advance and then take the test at a designated site in any of over 150 countries including the United States. Section reliabilities range from .86 to .90; reliability for the total exam is .95. These high reliability figures suggest that the TOEFL is quite an accurate measurement device.

The listening section consists of three parts: The first provides a series of oral statements, each followed by four multiple-choice paraphrases or explana-

27

tions of what was said. The second presents short conversations between two speakers, followed by an oral question on the conversation. The third part of the listening section includes announcements, lecture excerpts, and longer conversations; each is followed by several oral questions. Printed options are presented for all three parts of the listening section.

The second section, Structure and Written Expression, is based on academic writing and consists of two parts. The first part evaluates grammar mastery by having students select the best multiple-choice completion for sentences from which a word or phrase has been deleted. The second part consists of sentences, each of which has four words or phrases underlined; the examinee identifies which portion is unacceptable in standard written English.

The third section, Vocabulary and Reading Comprehension, is also divided into two parts. Sentences in the first part have a word or phrase underlined. Students demonstrate vocabulary mastery by selecting the multiple-choice option closest in meaning to the underlined portion. The reading comprehension part consists of academic passages, each followed by questions on the meaning of the passage.

Adjuncts to the TOEFL include the Test of Written English (TWE) and the Test of Spoken English (TSE); a released version of TSE is the Speaking Proficiency English Assessment Kit (SPEAK). Each of these tests will be discussed below and in later chapters. Educational Testing Service (ETS) also produces a pre-TOEFL exam, the Secondary Level English Proficiency Test (SLEP), and a non-academic ESL exam, the Test of English for International Communication (TOEIC).

Evaluation. The TOEFL has been criticized for its passive approach to language testing; that is, it requires no actual production of language at all, since it is all multiple-choice. Complaints have also been registered about the negative "backwash" effect of its all-objective format on instruction, which often results in ESL courses that focus only on the receptive skills tested by the TOEFL rather than language production. However, development of the TSE and TWE have tended to mute such concerns. Many have been critical of the fact that the TOEFL is a poor predictor of success in college. ETS has repeatedly pointed out that no English language proficiency test can, or ought to, be used to predict academic success since there is obviously more involved in academic success than just language proficiency. Others claim that the TOEFL is biased against certain language groups or majors in college, although major research reports do not substantiate such allegations. And still others hold that the TOEFL uses unrealistic, stilted language to trick foreign speakers of English. But these and other claims have been carefully evaluated and rebutted (Madsen, Haskell, and Stansfield 1988).

Despite the criticism of the TOEFL mentioned above, it is an effective measure of second-language proficiency in English. *Reviews of English Language Proficiency Tests* (Alderson, Krahnke, and Stansfield 1987) describes the

TOEFL as not only the most used but also the most researched of language tests, and "highly secure"; in short, "the best of its breed" (p. 81).

There are several factors that contribute to its stature. First, the TOEFL is jointly sponsored by some of the largest testing entities in the United States: the College Board (CB), the Graduate Record Examinations Board (GRE), and Educational Testing Service. Second, the structure of the TOEFL governing agency helps assure continuing input from the ESL teaching and testing profession. The fifteen-member TOEFL Policy Council includes CB and GRE representatives as well as leaders in higher education and ESL. The six-member TOEFL Research Committee consists of research specialists from the profession. And the six-member TOEFL Committee of Examiners consists of ESL professionals, who interact with specialists from the TOEFL program.

In addition, the TOEFL is committed to a continuous, intensive research agenda. The research arm of the TOEFL has produced 27 TOEFL reports during the past decade at an average cost of $75,000 per study; 22 additional research studies are under way or under consideration. This effort is complemented by TOEFL/ETS joint preparation of and commitment to a new "Code of Fair Testing Practices in Education."

Yet one more reason for acceptance of the TOEFL is the variety of services offered to examinees and institutions. These range from a new TOEFL Instructional Program (TIP), sample tapes, and booklets with advice on preparing for the TOEFL, to research reports, score verification, and various manuals on TOEFL interpretation (ETS 1987).

The MELAB. The relatively new Michigan English Language Assessment Battery (MELAB) less than five years ago replaced the "Michigan battery"—the Michigan Test of English Language Proficiency (MTELP), the Michigan Test of Aural Comprehension (MTAC,) and the essay—which had been in use for three decades—the "grandparent" of U.S. ESL examinations. Like its predecessor, the MELAB incorporates an essay as an integral part of the overall battery. And like the "old" Michigan, it includes a listening section, though one that is now enhanced by some discourse-level material (i.e., paragraph-length texts) such as is found on the TOEFL. The third section bears some resemblance to the earlier MTELP, but includes several enhancements, described below.

Like the TOEFL, the MELAB is not for sale; one must register to take the exam at an official testing site: (only the old, nonsecure MTELP and MTAC may be purchased, given, and scored locally). The MELAB is available in 120 countries worldwide, with 16 group centers in the United States and Canada. Unlike the TOEFL, with its 12 fixed administrations dates annually, the MELAB is offered at varying times and dates. Candidates can take the test a maximum of three times a year, but they must wait a minimum of six weeks before retaking it. As with the TOEFL, MELAB scoring is handled in-house; all scoring and score reporting is processed by the English Language Institute at the University of Michigan (ELI-UM).

Description. The MELAB is a three-part exam: Part 1 is a composition; Part 2 consists of a listening test or an optional oral rating; and Part 3 is a multiple-section objective test. The time required to take the test is approximately two and a half hours (30 minutes for Part 1, 25 minutes for Part 2, and 75 minutes for Part 3). Acceptable admissions scores tend to range from 75 to 85 on a 100-point scale; many institutions reportedly require additional ESL coursework for students with scores below 85.

Part 1 is a 30-minute essay. Unlike the TOEFL's TWE (Test of Written English), the MELAB provides two essay topics and students select one of these to write on. It is suggested that they write a 200- to 300-word composition; they are informed that they will lose credit if they write fewer than 150 words. Either a formal or informal style is acceptable, and the essay is scored holistically by two examiners; that is, each scorer reads the essay and gives it an overall score on a 10-point scale. (See Chapter Seven for a discussion of holistic scoring.)

Part 2 consists of 40 to 50 listening comprehension items, of three different types. The first group consists of items like those on the old MTAC—statements or questions (presented on a tape player); the candidate listens to the prompt and chooses the appropriate paraphrase or response. The second group involves an innovative testing strategy: statements and questions are presented with a special emphasis (e.g., contrastive stress, "I thought *John* wanted the apple pie..."). Examinees must choose either what the speaker would say next, or what an appropriate response would be. The final type of items consists of a lecture and a conversation. These discuss graphs or charts found in the examinees' answer sheet. Note taking is permitted. About twenty questions are presented in this third section of the listening comprehension subtest. In the total listening subtest, a 100-point scoring scale is used.

Part 3 of the MELAB consists of grammar items, a cloze reading test (i.e., a reading passage with words systematically deleted that candidates must replace), vocabulary, and reading. This 100-item subtest begins with 30 four-option, multiple-choice, sentence-completion grammar questions. The stem consists of a two-line written dialogue; candidates complete the second sentence by selecting the appropriate word or phrase from printed options.

The cloze portion of Part 3 presents a single prose selection with 20 words deleted. Candidates must replace the missing words by choosing from multiple-choice options (four per blank).

The vocabulary portion consists of 30 lexical items. These are presented in two formats. One utilizes a sentence from which a word has been deleted; candidates select the best of four multiple-choice options. The other format consists of a sentence with the key word underlined; candidates select the appropriate synonym. The reading comprehension portion of Part 3 includes approximately four academically-oriented prose passages, with an average of five four-option multiple-choice questions per passage.

Since the MELAB was created, approximately 50 topics have been developed for the Part 1 essay section. There are three forms of the listening part, and there are four forms of Part 3. An optional MELAB oral interview is also available on demand.

Evaluation. The MELAB is the only major commercial ESL placement test produced in the United States that incorporates an actual written composition as an integral part of the exam battery. This enhances the surface appeal of the test and places a commendable emphasis on an important language skill. The discourse-level material included in the new listening section is an important improvement over the old battery, as is the new discourse-level material in Part 3, namely the cloze.

It is reassuring to know that the essay is scored by two readers, that note taking is permitted on part of the listening subtest, and that multiple reading passages are still used in order to guard against possible topic bias.

But in what ways might the MELAB be improved? First, there is a need for more recent information on the validation of the test, as well as reliability statistics. ELI-UM has recently published a new information bulletin on the MELAB (ELI 1989) and plans to introduce a new technical manual in 1990. Additionally, just as we hear in the computer field of "IBM-compatible" wares, so it would be helpful to have "TOEFL-compatible" information—current studies showing the equivalence of MELAB and TOEFL scores.

Second, it would be useful to specify just what Part 3 of the MELAB is actually testing, since users of the battery are encouraged to use part-scores in addition to the total score. At first glance, it appears that the new Michigan battery measures the four skills of listening, reading, writing, and (on the optional MELAB oral interview) speaking. But the actual content of Part 3 includes grammar, vocabulary, reading, and a cloze, and very likely measures general English proficiency. There is nothing objectionable, of course, about assessing general proficiency in English, but users could profit from knowing how to interpret this single Part 3 subscore. Conceivably the test might be modified (as the TOEFL was a few years ago), so that a separate reading comprehension score could be provided, as well as a grammar or general proficiency score.

Despite these areas which deserve attention, the MELAB appears to be a secure and sound placement examination.

The "Old Michigan Battery"—MTELP and MTAC. Various retired forms of the old Michigan placement battery are available for purchase. The "Michigan Test of English Language Proficiency" (MTELP) is the forerunner of the new MELAB Part 3, and the "Michigan Test of Aural Comprehension" (MTAC) is the forerunner of the MELAB listening subtest. At the outset, however, we strongly recommend against using these for placement purposes. In fact, an official University of Michigan bulletin recently indicated that these retired subtests (the MTELP and MTAC) are not considered adequate for initial admissions screening purposes, as they do not constitute the entire battery; moreover, they may not be secure. They can be useful to institutions for measuring student progress through ESL instructional programs.

Description. Since these subtests from the old Michigan battery are not recommended for placement purposes, only a very brief description will be provided. The MTELP is an all-objective test of grammar, vocabulary, and reading comprehension. The structure and vocabulary portions each contain 40 items, and the reading comprehension section 20 items. The actual testing time required for this four-option multiple-choice test is 75 minutes.

The MTAC is a listening test consisting of tape-recorded statements and questions. There are three forms of this 30-minute test; students respond to multiple-choice printed options to questions involving appropriate response and paraphrase.

Evaluation. A careful review of the MTELP by Jenks (1987) challenges the test's lack of security and weak validation data. Subsection scores (notably that of reading) need to be used with caution, since the three parts are not timed separately, and therefore students taking the exam for the first time may not finish a given section; this can result in a spuriously low score for that part. A review of the MTAC (Jones 1987) suggests it has more of a grammar emphasis than a listening comprehension focus. It should be noted as well that this listening test consists entirely of discrete, sentence-level utterances. The MTELP, on the other hand, does have some discourse-level material, namely in the reading comprehension section.

In spite of such problems, these 30-year-old tests are still very popular. To the extent that candidates do not have access to the tests, they still provide a fairly good measure of general proficiency. Again, however, it should be emphasized that they should no longer be used for admissions purposes and serve their most appropriate function as on-campus tests.

The CELT. The Comprehensive English Language Test (CELT) was developed by David P. Harris and Leslie A. Palmer. This commercially available placement test (also intended for use as a progress test) is available through McGraw-Hill.

Description. The CELT contains three sections—listening, structure, and vocabulary. Section 1 is a 40-minute listening comprehension subtest. This 50-item, tape-recorded section consists of three parts. The first of these presents 20 oral questions, primarily "what, where, when, and who" types of questions; examinees select appropriate responses from four-option printed choices in their answer booklets. The second part consists of 20 oral statements; examinees select an appropriate paraphrase from four-option printed choices. The third part presents ten dialogues (each consisting of a single exchange between a man and a woman); a third voice asks a question about the dialogue. Candidates select an appropriate answer from four printed options.

Section 2, the grammar portion, consists of 75 multiple-choice sentence-completion items. The format for this 45-minute section is the same as that of the grammar section presented on the MELAB: short two-line printed dialogues have a word or phrase missing from the second line; examinees choose one of four printed options to complete the sentence.

The 75-item vocabulary section consists of two parts; 35 minutes is the allocated time. The first part presents 35 sentence-completion items, each with four-option choices. The second part presents 40 very short definitions, each followed by four lexical options from which the item being defined is chosen.

Evaluation. Like the TOEFL and MTELP, the CELT has been in use for a couple of decades. However, little information is available other than that which appeared in the 1970 "Technical Manual," and current validation studies are needed. A more immediate need is the development of additional test forms (at present only two are available, the second of which appeared for the first time in 1986).

This all-objective instrument would be enhanced by measures of productive tasks, such as writing and speaking. Moreover, the test sorely needs to evaluate discourse-level listening and reading matter. In short, the test is somewhat dated. Nevertheless, what it does, which is to test grammar and vocabulary knowledge and listening ability, it does rather well.

A final crucial matter needs to be raised: like the present commercial versions of the MTELP and MTAC, the CELT can no longer be assumed secure. Therefore, one needs to be very cautious in assuming that CELT scores invariably represent a student's actual language ability. Use of the instrument should probably be limited to decisions less crucial than university admission—for example, progress in an ESL course.

The ALI/GU. Another U.S. ESL placement test battery in common use is the so-called "ALI/GU"—the official name of which is Tests of English as a Second Language of the American Language Institute, Georgetown University. This prominent old battery has been replaced at Georgetown by an in-house instrument, the ALI/GU EPT (ALI/GU English Proficiency Test).

The ALI/GU battery (prior to 1961 known as the AULC tests, since they were developed at the American University Language Center) was developed for the U.S. Agency for International Development (USAID) and the International Communication Agency (ICA). The tests were used overseas to screen foreign applicants for USAID and ICA training programs, and were used at Georgetown for placing students at the ALI. The ALI/GU has been officially retired; ALI policy is that it is no longer viewed as a secure test and should not be given or accepted as proof of proficiency in English. The new ALI/GU EPT is given by USAID offices to candidates for scholarships, and at the ALI, and university admissions officers may occasionally receive score reports from this test. The ALI/GU EPT is quite different from the ALI/GU (it is not a battery of tests, for example, but rather a single instrument with sections similar to those of the TOEFL), and ALI/GU EPT scores should not be interpreted as if they were ALI/GU scores. The ALI/GU EPT has been equated to the TOEFL, and the American Language Institute at Georgetown University can assist in score interpretation. Since neither the old ALI/GU nor the new ALI/GU EPT are commercially available, they will not be discussed further here.

Other Tests. A variety of other instruments are occasionally used in making placement decisions, particularly at "easier than TOEFL" levels. These include the Secondary Level English Proficiency Test (SLEP), designed for foreign students in grades 7 to 12; the English Language Skills Assessment (ELSA), which is primarily a test of reading proficiency; Structure Tests—English Language (STEL), a series of grammar tests designed to complement ELSA; and the Test of English Proficiency Level (TEPL), designed to place students at any of seven levels, ranging from "no English" to "high advanced." These tests are really not satisfactory for measuring the second-language proficiency of students about to embark on a college-level course of studies. Some ESL exams such as the Ilyin Oral Interview (IOI) or even the Literacy Skills section of the Basic English Skills Test (BEST) are also simply too basic. The well-constructed Test of English for International Communication (TOEIC) appears to do well what it was intended for—assessing English competence for a work context—but there is no evidence that it can do double duty as an academic placement test. Similarly, neither the Scholastic Aptitude Test (SAT) nor the Graduate Records Examination (GRE) can be expected to provide appropriate information about a foreign student's English proficiency.

ESL Tests Used for Special Purposes: Speaking Proficiency

Some commercial ESL tests are used for special purposes in the admissions process. A department of statistics may need to assess the oral English skills of foreign graduate students who are applying to teach as graduate assistants. A department of journalism or business may need to have a good measure of foreign students' writing ability. This final section of the chapter will discuss these two requirements—the need to assess speaking and writing proficiency.

We will look first at instruments designed to evaluate the speaking proficiency of foreign university students, notably those who might serve as teaching assistants (TAs).

The TSE. The Test of Spoken English is a speaking test produced by TOEFL staff at Educational Testing Service. Administered 10 to 12 times annually at official TOEFL sites, the TSE does not use a live examiner; questions are cued by a tape plus a test booklet, and testees' responses are tape-recorded. The number of candidates taking the exam has increased from 192 in the initial administration (October 1979) to about 15,000 during the 1988-89 academic year. A new set of questions is created for each test administration. Scores for overall comprehensibility range from 0 to 300; in addition, diagnostic scores in the areas of pronunciation, grammar, and fluency are reported—each of these ranging from 0 to 3. The test takes about 20 minutes to complete.

Description. The TSE is divided into seven sections. The first section, which is not scored, is a warm-up; students are asked open-ended questions about themselves. Section 2 requires candidates to read a paragraph aloud; scores are based on pronunciation, fluency, and comprehensibility. Section 3 has examinees complete sentences such as "When the library opens. . . ." Scoring is based on grammar and comprehensibility. In Section 4, a series of pictures is presented and respondents are asked to tell the story depicted. Here, pronunciation, grammar, fluency, and comprehensibility are evaluated. Section 5 consists of a single picture depicting some sort of accident or problem. Four questions are asked about the situation. Here, again, pronunciation, grammar, fluency, and comprehensibility are scored. The next section has candidates handle three questions requiring two types of task: one, description of an object; and two, discussion of their opinions on contemporary topics of interest. In this part, pronunciation, fluency, and comprehensibility are evaluated. The final section requires examinees to study a printed schedule or notice and then explain the contents in some detail. Again, pronunciation, fluency, and comprehensibility are checked.

Evaluation. First, the relatively high cost of taking the test is worrisome to many ($75 in 1989-90, due to increase to $95 in 1990-91). And critics of the TSE have been concerned about the semidirect nature of the test, which does not allow for student interaction with a live examiner (Bailey 1987). Some have expressed concern about certain portions of the exam: The completion of discrete sentences (Section 3) does not seem sufficiently communicative; some students with reasonable proficiency have difficulty with the Section 6 description task (e.g., describe a bicycle); and some appear to do better than anticipated in Section 7 (which has students explain a schedule) by simply reading information from the printed page. The three latter concerns are currently under discussion at ETS; it appears likely that appropriate modifications will be forthcoming.

Nevertheless, the TSE is generally applauded for its value in screening foreign students who are being considered as teaching assistants. Tasks such as reading a paragraph aloud, paraphrasing, and making extemporaneous explanations (together with evaluation that ranges from pronunciation to general intelligibility) have been found appropriate for identifying TAs with the requisite skills for their assignment.

In addition, the TSE has been field-tested in evaluating foreign teaching assistants. The correlation between students' rating of foreign TAs' "overall ability to communicate in English" and performance on the TSE was an impressive .78. In addition, interrater reliability coefficients for the four TSE scores of comprehensibility, pronunciation, grammar, and fluency ranged from .77 to .85. Clark and Swinton (1980) indicate that these are "probable underestimates," since operationally TSE scores are based on the average of two separate ratings for each paper (p. 43). Finally, the exam is secure and available worldwide ten times a year.

The SPEAK Test. Educational Testing Service has made retired forms of the TSE available for local purchase. Labeled the Speaking Proficiency English Assessment Kit (SPEAK), the test includes the same seven sections described above under the TSE. This $300 kit includes 30 test books, reel-to-reel and cassette test tapes, rating sheets, test booklets (visual stimulus material), directions for administering the test, and materials for the training of raters. ETS indicates that raters can prepare themselves adequately in two to three days. Additional forms are available for $100 each.

Institutional purchase of SPEAK can relieve students of the high cost of taking the TSE oral interview, and can facilitate the rapid reporting of student performance. It is reassuring that four different forms of the SPEAK are available. The principal concern, as with any off-the-shelf exam, is that of test security.

The MELAB Oral Rating. Also available in conjunction with the MELAB is an optional oral interview. This consists of a live interaction with a local examiner. It is given on demand when a local examiner is available; close to one thousand interviews are administered annually at a minimal cost per interview. A four-point evaluation scale is used, with proficiency descriptions for each level accompanying the score report.

Description. Candidates are evaluated on this scale (ranging from poor facility with the language to virtual native proficiency) in terms of their overall oral/aural ability. In addition, four subscores are reported: (1) grammatical accuracy and range, (2) vocabulary, (3) pronunciation, and (4) understanding. After completing these ratings, interviewers provide these general assessments: (1) whether the candidate is sufficiently proficient to pursue college study without additional training in English; (2) if not, whether the candidate is ready for part-time academic study plus an ESL course; and (3) whether the candidate is proficient enough to teach at an American university.

In generating the five scores referred to above (the overall rating plus four diagnostic subscores), examiners make judgments based on a rating grid. For example, a person with level-1 proficiency in pronunciation "can be understood only with considerable difficulty," while a person with level-3 pronunciation "may have a noticeable foreign accent but it generally does not hinder communication."

Evaluation. Little published information is available from which an evaluation can be made. However, a few observations are possible. Unlike the TSE, local live examiners are used. This enhances face validity but limits the availability of the exam. Moreover, reliability data are needed to assure users of score consistency, particularly since only a single rater is used in scoring the interviews. The only training local examiners receive is a set of printed instructions. Michigan realizes the need for more training material, including sample tapes, and an improved training procedure is planned. The cost of the interview is minimal—a mere $5.

This open-ended MELAB oral interview is more communicative than the TSE (though undoubtedly less reliable). While various commercial tests of listening (or reading, for that matter) are very similar in format and content, there is a dramatic difference between the ETS and Michigan speaking exams. It is beneficial to the profession and to institutions of higher learning that these alternatives are available.

Other Speaking Tests. The most promising alternative to the tests described above is the Oral Proficiency Interview (OPI), initiated by the American Council on the Teaching of Foreign Languages (ACTFL), Educational Testing Service, and the U.S. government-affiliated Interagency Language Roundtable. The OPI is an interview procedure that requires extensive and rigorous training and examiner certification.

Though expensive and time-consuming, the ten-level rating system is based on sound psychometric concepts. It involves communicative interaction tailored to the ability level of each candidate. It investigates examinees' ability to function in the language as well as their accuracy and social appropriateness. While the OPI is being employed more and more extensively in university foreign language programs, only a relatively small number of ESL examiners have been certified to date. For this reason, a full description and evaluation will not be provided in this chapter.

As a final note, numerous bilingual tests using a speaking modality have been developed, but none were really designed to screen students for university placement. Many look at language dominance; some instruments evaluate general proficiency, student readiness to read, work interests, and even intelligence or personality. One of the more prominent language dominance tests is the advanced "Bilingual Syntax Measure" (BSM II). Designed for grades 3 to 12, BSM II is occasionally used on the college level for experimental research.

For a detailed discussion of oral proficiency testing for international teaching assistants, see Chapter Seven.

ESL Tests Used for Special Purposes: Writing Proficiency

For a variety of reasons, there are more specialized tests of speaking than of writing. For one thing, commercial tests tend to include either a direct or indirect measure of writing as an integral component of the battery. Many institutions that do not depend on subscores of such tests often feel capable of producing and scoring their own test of writing. In a recent survey of 521 institutions of higher learning, Ross (1988) found that 48 percent require a writing test of incoming non-native speakers of English. Three-fourths of these use an in-house test or a system-wide test such as the California State University English Placement Test. Among those using a writing measure, approximately 15 percent of the undergraduate institutions use the Michigan Test and 9 percent some other test, such as SAT's "Test of Standard Written English."

The TWE. TOEFL's Test of Written English (TWE) is presently the only "stand alone" commercial ESL test of writing produced in the United States. Introduced in 1986, the TWE has been administered with the TOEFL—as of this writing—eight times (with sixteen different topics) to 260,000 examinees. The topic types used are based on a study of academic writing required in 190 university departments (Bridgeman and Carlson 1983). Like the basic (multiple-choice) TOEFL, the TWE is not available for purchase. It is offered worldwide during four of the TOEFL's dozen annual administrations.

Description. The TWE presently draws upon two topic types: (1) compare and contrast two opposing points of view and take a position; or (2) describe and interpret a chart or graph. No topic is ever reused. Candidates are allowed 30 minutes to organize, write, and edit their essay.

Grading is holistic; readers evaluate the writing for "overall communicative effectiveness." ESL and English composition specialists at American and Canadian universities and secondary schools are trained as readers. They use a six-point scale devised by composition professionals—"6" being near-native proficiency and "1" containing "serious and persistent" writing problems. Each paper is read independently by two readers; their scores are totaled and then averaged. Any pair of scores differing by more than one point results in the use of a third reader—in every case a senior "reading manager."

Evaluation. It is difficult to conceive of a more carefully prepared and executed examination than the TWE. It is based on extensive research related to the writing required in institutions of higher learning. Some of the most respected composition professionals in the country are involved in directing the program. These specialists ("core readers") meet regularly to design and select topics, of which eight to ten are normally selected from a pool of about 50; these are then revised and pretested both within the United States and outside the country to determine whether or not they "work" with a variety of non-native speakers of English.

Readers are carefully trained; those not able to perform with accuracy and consistency are not invited to become part of the reader pool. The use of two readers for each essay is commendable, since it increases overall reliability (reliabilities for two readers range from .85 to .88).

The TOEFL is totally subsidizing the TWE at present. In addition, many tens of thousands of dollars are being spent on TWE research. It would be helpful to colleges and universities if the TWE could be "factored" in to the total TOEFL score and administered at every TOEFL administration. But this is not economically feasible under the present fee structure. In the meantime, it is to be hoped that institutions of higher learning will avail themselves of this extraordinary resource. A detailed discussion of the TWE and its interpretation can be found in Chapter Six.

Summary and Conclusion

A relatively small number of U.S.-produced tests are presently being used for general placement of non-native speakers of English in American colleges and universities. The vast majority of U.S. institutions of higher learning require the TOEFL but will often accept the MELAB, and sometimes the CELT, ALI/GU EPT, or MTELP/MTAC.

The TOEFL is undoubtedly the most thoroughly researched and most carefully analyzed ESL/EFL examination in the world. Moreover, it undergoes constant revision and enhancement. While it has been assessed as "the best of its breed," and although it has been enhanced in recent years by adjunct tests of writing and speaking, it needs a direct measure of proficiency (such as the TWE) integrated into the basic test. This will help assure that the numerous institutions relying on the TOEFL have access to the most sound total measure of language proficiency possible, as well as needed diagnostic information.

The MELAB is a respectable alternative to the TOEFL. This "new Michigan test" incorporates an essay, and it provides, as the TOEFL does, for an optional speaking evaluation. Moreover, it is secure. The principal need is for more research and validation of this still relatively new battery.

The all multiple-choice CELT provides a more limited assessment than either the TOEFL or MELAB and their adjunct tests supply. It was a sound test when it was created years ago, but has scarcely been revised since then. And like any off-the-shelf test, it lacks the security of tests like the TOEFL and MELAB. However, the CELT is an option for those needing a commercial test that can be scored locally. Competing with the CELT are retired forms of the Michigan—the MTELP and the MTAC—providing a measure of structure, vocabulary, and reading, and a measure of listening comprehension, respectively.

For the placement of students substantially under the usual 500 TOEFL score, there is a need for a well-developed battery. At present there is scarcely anything in place except the TEPL; and this test is lacking in basic statistical verification. In the interim, separate tests such as the ELSA and STEL as well as "borrowed" secondary school tests like the SLEP are being used for lower-proficiency students.

To meet the needs of individual departments and programs requiring specific assessments of a particular skill, subtests and sometimes specialized examinations are available. One such need is that of assessing the speaking proficiency of graduate teaching assistants from overseas. The most widely used ESL speaking test for placement purposes in America is the TSE/SPEAK. Also used is the optional MELAB interview. The most frequently administered commercial ESL writing test in America is the carefully researched TWE. A somewhat distant second is the MELAB essay. At the present, however, the use of in-house essays is by far the most prevalent means of assessing this subskill for placement purposes. A discussion of procedures for on-campus writing tests is provided in Chapter Six.

While nearly all of the U.S. ESL exams discussed here appear to be sound and well conceived, they tend towards the conservative. One would hope that more communicative features of language use might begin to be incorporated into tests. But there is a more immediate need: too many tests are lacking careful statistical evaluation. Notably absent in the case of most speaking and writing tests are interrater reliability estimates. And even basic validation information is often unavailable.

Yet there is much to be commended: Educational Testing Service, sponsor of the giant TOEFL exam, is expending great sums on research and reaching widely into the ESL profession for direction. Despite the half million examinees processed annually, the TOEFL now has a bona fide writing test; moreover, steady improvements are planned involving the listening section and other parts of the TOEFL and the TSE. The MELAB reflects important changes at Michigan, such as a much stronger listening subtest. The MELAB, ELSA, and other tests are giving cloze a try. The SLEP (though not technically a college test) is creative in the use of visuals and maps. And although the TEPL is essentially unverified statistically at this point, it is imaginative in testing such skills as writing. U.S. tests are becoming more and more committed to measuring students' abilities to handle longer stretches of language, and to providing direct measures of skills such as speaking and writing. While still on the conservative side, U.S. tests appear to be gradually incorporating communicative insights from the ESL profession at large. For more information on English language tests, see the list of addresses in appendix A.

5
British Tests of English As a Foreign Language
J. Charles Alderson

Recent British Council surveys (The British Council 1985 and 1988) of the tests and examinations accepted by British universities, polytechnics, and colleges as evidence of proficiency in English as a second or foreign language (The British Council 1985 and 1988) have revealed a wide range of instruments acceptable to British admissions officers. More than 37 tests and examinations are recorded in those surveys. Twelve British tests of EFL/ESL are reviewed in Alderson, Krahnke, and Stansfield (1988). However, by far the most widely accepted proficiency tests in the United Kingdom are (1) the British Council–University of Cambridge Local Examinations Syndicate's English Language Testing Service Test (ELTS); (2) the Cambridge Syndicate's own Certificate of Proficiency in English as a Foreign Language (CPE); and (3) the Educational Testing Service's TOEFL. Relevant figures from the 1988 survey are shown in Table 1.

Despite the relative familiarity among British academics with the TOEFL, there is much less awareness in the United States of the British equivalents. It is hoped that this chapter will provide information that will prove both interesting and useful to those less familiar with British tests of proficiency in EFL/ESL.

The British Examination System

By way of introduction, it is important that the reader understand that there are considerable differences in testing practice and traditions between the United States and the United Kingdom that affect the way tests are produced, validated, interpreted, and accepted. Most U.K. tests are produced by examination boards, officially nonprofit institutions whose main role within the U.K. education system is to produce syllabuses, or programs of study, and examinations for those syllabuses for the measurement of school achievement, most notably at the ages of 15/16 and 17/18. Examinations for the former age group of school pupils are known as Ordinary or O-Level exams, and those for the latter age

TABLE 1
NUMBER OF INSTITUTIONS RECOGNIZING
ENGLISH LANGUAGE QUALIFICATIONS FOR ENTRANCE REQUIREMENTS

	CPE 1985	CPE 1988	TOEFL 1985	TOEFL 1988	ELTS 1985	ELTS 1988
Universities, associated institutions, and hospitals	56	63	45	64	46	72
Polytechnics	7	22	1	20	7	22
Higher education, further education, and arts and technology	56	67	28	49	31	54

group are known as Advanced or A-Level exams. (The Scottish system is somewhat different, but as this does not affect tests of EFL/ESL, no reference to such differences will be made.) U.K. universities and colleges accept students on the basis of their achievement in O- and A-Level exams, and as might be expected, different departments in different institutions have varying entry requirements. The most usual requirement, however, for university-level study is for three relevant subjects at A-Level and several at O-Level, the latter usually but not always including English and Math. Scores at O-Level are reported as letter grades, ranging from A to G (U is "unclassified," and X is "failed to appear"). At A-Level, scores are currently reported on a scale from A to F.

Currently, the examination boards are grouped on a regional basis, and each of the five regional groups includes boards that are connected to particular universities. Thus, the Northern Examining Authority includes the Joint Matriculation Board (representing the universities of Manchester, Liverpool, Leeds, Sheffield, and Birmingham); the Midland Examining Group includes the University of Cambridge Local Examinations Syndicate; and so on. Most of these regional groups also produce examinations intended to measure proficiency in English as a second or foreign language.

In addition to these school-oriented examination boards, there are also vocationally and professionally oriented examining bodies, some of which, like the London Chamber of Commerce, the Royal Society of Arts, and Trinity House, also produce tests of proficiency in EFL/ESL. However, not all of these, as the British Council surveys cited above show, are regarded as acceptable evidence of EFL proficiency by U.K. institutions of higher education. This is not to suggest that their examinations are notably inferior, but simply to indicate that they are not currently regarded as appropriate or validated instruments for assessing EFL/ESL proficiency for those students who wish to undertake studies in English-medium institutions. Indeed, some of the examinations produced by these boards—most notably those of the Royal Society of Arts—are highly regarded by the U.K. EFL teaching profession, are interestingly innovative, and have had considerable influence on language testing practice more widely than the shores of the United Kingdom.

British Test Development

In addition to the organization of examining bodies, the way in which tests are produced and validated in the United Kingdom differs significantly from normal practice in the United States. A brief description of this is contained in the introduction to Alderson, Krahnke, and Stansfield (1987):

> The examinations produced by these exam boards are not standardized or normed in the usual sense, but are produced and administered for one occasion only. Thus tests (often known as papers) produced for administration in Spring 1987 will never be used again. . . . Indeed, past papers are often made publicly available, sometimes for a small fee.
>
> Due to the constant need to produce new examinations and the lack of emphasis by exam boards on the need for empirical rather than judgmental validation, these examinations are rarely, if ever, tried out on pupils or subjected to the statistical analyses of typical test production procedures. Examination boards do not see the need to pretest and validate their instruments, nor conduct posthoc analyses of their tests' performance. Although the objective items in the tests are usually pretested, the statistics are rarely published. . . . This is not to say that the tests produced are not valid and reliable, but that we have very little empirical evidence of their characteristics.
>
> Rather, the exam boards lay great store by the asserted validity of their examination construction procedures, which rely almost exclusively upon 'expert' judgments. The production of a test for any occasion is the responsibility of a chief examiner, selected by the board for 'proven' qualities of judgment and track record of reliability of marking [examination answers] . . . in past years. This chief examiner will also have recent, if not current, experience teaching the subject for which he or she is producing a test. The chief examiner is aided by a set of assistant examiners and a moderating committee who produce, scrutinize, edit, and finalize the tests (a process known as moderation). In addition, the chief examiner produces marking criteria (sometimes known as *mark schemes*) and is responsible, with senior examiners, for the training and standardizing of markers and the checking of interrater reliability after the examination has been

administered. Even in this process of the checking of interrater reliability, it is extremely unusual for an exam board to calculate or publish statistics of the reliability of its markers . . . . The exam boards place great faith in the qualities of their chief examiners and in their selection, moderation, standardization, and grade-awarding procedures (Alderson in Alderson et al. 1987, 3).

One of the main problems with such a test construction process is that the examination boards never know whether any one year's "paper" is equivalent to tests given in previous years. For this reason, the boards engage in elaborate "grade-awarding" procedures that are intended, as far as possible, to ensure the equivalence of test results over the years. Such procedures tend to rely rather heavily upon the assumption that the test-taking population does not change from year to year. While this may be true for the large numbers of school-leavers taking O-Levels (although there are good reasons to doubt this, too), it is less obviously so for the more heterogeneous populations of students taking EFL/ESL tests. (See Chapter Eight for a discussion of validity, reliability, and equivalent forms.)

There are, however, one or two notable exceptions to the practice of test construction described above, and the most significant of these is the English Language Testing Service Test (ELTS), jointly produced by the University of Cambridge Local Examinations Syndicate and the British Council. Unlike most other U.K. EFL examinations, which, as described, are administered once only and rarely trial-tested, the ELTS test is a secure test that has been trial-tested, extensively validated, and is in widespread international use. The current ELTS Revision Project (discussed below) is engaged in piloting and trying out a new battery of tests, as well as a series of test production procedures that will ensure that parallel forms of the new test are produced annually and adequately pretested and validated before they are used operationally. This will also ensure that the equivalence of parallel forms of the test is established in advance. It may be that the innovation in test construction and validation procedures represented by the development of the ELTS test will have an impact on test construction, validation, and interpretation rather more generally in U.K. EFL/ESL exams.

Comparisons Among British Tests

The proliferation in the United Kingdom of different examinations in EFL/ESL has long been seen as something of a problem, since there have been no means of relating the different exams to each other. Although language teachers have often developed a sense of the relative ease and difficulty of some exams, such a sense is largely intuitive, personal, incomplete across the range of exams offered, and not, to date, subject to empirical testing. How, for example, does a grade C on Cambridge's First Certificate in English relate to the award of Intermediate on the RSA's Communicative Use of English as a Foreign Language exam? Is a B in Cambridge's Certificate of Proficiency in English the equivalent of Band 6.5 on ELTS? How does a pass on the ARELS Diploma exam relate to performance on ETS's Test of Spoken English? Questions such as these abound, and the confusion is made worse by the fact that most exam boards report scores in terms that may be internally consistent but neither compare easily with the scales of other boards nor relate directly or easily to performance in the real world. Obviously the question of comparability of standards is complex, given the diversity of formats that the different examinations have developed over the years. It is at least plausible that different exams test different aspects of linguistic and communicative competence, and that therefore direct comparisons are impossible in principle. Nevertheless, there has grown over the years a feeling that however impossible such a comparison may be, it should be attempted in order to help the users of test scores—students, teachers, admissions officers, and the like—to begin to make sense of a confusing situation. As a result, the English Speaking Union is currently completing a Framework Project (Carroll and West 1989) which has involved developing a series of "yardsticks" or scales on which the most common U.K. exams can be plotted empirically.

The English Speaking Union Framework Project. Central to the ESU Framework is the "yardstick." A yardstick is a descriptive scale of language performance. The yardsticks contain nine levels or bands, with associated descriptive statements that aim to outline the principal characteristics of the performance that can be expected of a student at that level. These descriptors are intended to be interpretable in terms of real-world performance, so that they can be readily understood and used by "lay" people. The yardsticks are intended to be used as a framework on which all examinations can be plotted. The aim is to allow examinations and their components to be described in common terms and to be compared indirectly, even if the content of the tests differs from exam to exam.

Carroll and West (1989) present the detailed descriptions for 22 yardsticks, each containing 9 different levels. The yardsticks are as follows:

Yardstick

1 Overall language proficiency
2 Oral proficiency
3 Graphic proficiency
4 Listening
5 Speaking
6 Reading
7 Writing
8 Listening for social and personal purposes
9 Listening for business purposes

10 Listening for study/training purposes
11 Speaking for social and personal purposes
12 Speaking for business purposes
13 Speaking for study/training purposes
14 Reading for social and personal purposes
15 Reading for business purposes
16 Reading for study/training purposes
17 Writing for social and personal purposes
18 Writing for business purposes
19 Writing for study/training purposes
20 Linguistic skills
21 Functional skills
22 Examination skills

All yardsticks, the authors claim, have been built up in a consistent way out of three elements. These are: the nine levels, a description of task difficulty (or "Input"), and a description of expected candidate performance (or "Output").

Associated with the yardsticks is a "Chart of English Language Examinations from Britain" that plots the different grade levels or scores of the various tests and examinations surveyed against Yardstick 1—Overall language proficiency. It is thus possible to roughly compare at a glance the results of a wide range of British ESL/EFL examinations.

Construction of the framework and yardsticks proceeded in two phases: experts examined test forms produced by 16 U.K. examining authorities and classified the tasks and formats on "Fact Sheets," using common categories that were refined as a result of this process. Tests were described in terms of the performance activities in which candidates must engage and the enabling skills tapped by such activities. Task difficulties were estimated and described in terms of parameters like size, complexity, range, speed, and so on, and the expected performances were characterized according to parameters like relevance, accuracy, intelligibility, coherence, style, and so on. The levels of performance expected on each test were then plotted onto the common scale.

In addition, sample scripts and taped performances from each exam were obtained, and judged according to the nine-point yardstick. Those scripts and tapes where there was unanimity or near unanimity among judges were then sent to the examination boards, who were asked to rate them according to their normal procedures and criteria. The results should provide an empirical verification of how the different examinations can be related to common scales, and thereby to each other. The resultant publications (Carroll and West 1989; and the associated chart) should provide useful information for test users—candidates, employers, and educational institutions—as well as for teachers (to help them select an examination suited to their needs and to the levels of their students).

The Cambridge-TOEFL Comparability Study. The most internationally widespread EFL examinations are ETS's Test of English as a Foreign Language (TOEFL) and the University of Cambridge Local Examinations Syndicate's First Certificate in English and the Certificate of Proficiency in English. As the latter test (known as the CPE) is widely recognized in the United Kingdom for admissions purposes, it would seem to be useful to have some idea of how performance on the CPE relates to performance on the TOEFL (the First Certificate level of proficiency is unacceptable to virtually all U.K. universities and polytechnics). An interesting development, therefore, is the Cambridge Examinations-TOEFL Comparability Study, which started in 1987 and was scheduled to finish by the end of 1989. The aim of this project, directed by Lyle Bachman of the University of California, Los Angeles, is to compare the abilities measured by the two tests and to examine the equivalence of the test scores they generate.

The two test batteries represent radically different approaches to language test development, since the TOEFL is a prototypical psychometric, or "norm-referenced," test, whereas the CPE is constructed using the traditional British test construction procedures outlined above. The resultant study should be of practical interest both to test developers and to test users, as well as being of value to language testing researchers. For example, it will be interesting to see to what extent the two tests overlap in their coverage of skills and in their predictive abilities. However, since new versions of the CPE are not validated against previous forms of the test, it will be difficult to generalize from the results obtained from one version of the test to other, new versions. For this reason, it will still prove difficult to relate TOEFL scores to CPE scores. In any case, the TOEFL and the CPE are designed for different purposes, and indeed the scores they yield are often used for different purposes. The CPE, for example, is frequently used for teacher certification purposes in many countries. It may be, however, that this Comparability Study heralds the beginning of studies comparing U.K. and U.S. tests designed for the same purpose. The most obvious test to compare with the TOEFL from among the British tests is the ELTS test, since it, unlike the CPE, is designed specifically to assess the language skills of those applicants who wish to study in English-medium situations. Unlike the CPE, but like the TOEFL, the ELTS test is constructed along psychometric lines, is validated against a range of measures, and new versions are directly comparable to previous versions. Any comparison of the ELTS against the TOEFL, despite the differences in content between the two, is likely to yield more stable results. Such a study would be of particular interest, as the ELTS test is currently being redesigned.

The ELTS Revision Project

This project, set up in January 1987 by the British Council and the University of Cambridge Local Examinations Syndicate, is directed by J. Charles Alderson at the University of Lancaster. The revised test was designed and produced by a number of project teams in the United Kingdom, Australia, and Canada, and is administered by an international consortium, to be known as IELTS: the International English Language Testing System.

Feedback was gathered on the existing test from a wide range of test users, including receiving institutions, overseas test centers, subject specialists, language teachers and testers, and British Council officers, and this information has been added to an extensive validation study carried out at the University of Edinburgh (Criper and Davies, 1988; Hughes et al., 1988). As a result of this consultative process, the revised test has been designed, piloted, and tested in the United Kingdom, Australia, and elsewhere, and was introduced in fall 1989. New versions of the revised test will be produced internationally on an annual basis.

The revised test builds upon the established strengths of the existing test, while at the same time improving and streamlining it. The test has a general and a modular component, and the planned structure of these components is compared with the old ELTS as follows:

Old ELTS	New IELTS
General	
G1: Reading	G1: Listening
G2: Listening	G2: Speaking
Modular	
Five subject areas: Life Sciences, Medicine, Physical Sciences, Social Sciences, Technology, and General Academic	Three more broadly defined disciplinary groups: Modules A, B, and C
M1: Study Skills	M1: Reading
M2: Writing	M2: Writing
M3: Interview	

General Training
(For candidates whose training will be of a practical, technical nature and is largely workshop-based.)

Scores for those going on to academic study will continue to be reported on a nine-point Band scale, in profile form (Listening, Speaking, Reading, and Writing) as well as on an Overall Band Scale. New training and monitoring procedures will ensure the increased reliability of the scores on subjectively assessed test components, such as essays and oral interviews.

It is beyond the scope of this chapter to provide detailed descriptions of the wide range of British EFL examinations that U.S. admissions officers might encounter. Two recent publications provide excellent descriptions and reviews of these tests, however, and the interested reader is referred to them for further information. They are *The Pitman Guide*, edited by Susan Davies and Richard West, Longman, 1981; and *Reviews of English Language Proficiency Tests*, edited by J. C. Alderson, K. J. Krahnke, and C. W. Stansfield, Teachers of English to Speakers of Other Languages, 1987.

Further information can also be obtained from individual examination boards, whose addresses are given in appendix A.

Summary and Conclusion

The late 1980s have seen many interesting developments in the United Kingdom with respect to EFL/ESL examinations. Not only are the examining authorities beginning to adopt a more empirical approach to test validation, but they are also increasingly aware of the need to help the outside world understand what at first sight appears to be a confusing array of tests with different content, standards, and interpretations. Increased collaboration among examination boards is likely to mark future developments, and international collaboration, both in research, as on the Comparability Study, and in test development and administration, as on the ELTS Revision Project, is likely to mean that British EFL exams and their international counterparts will become more widespread, promoted, understood, and used. Thus it is likely to be particularly important for U.S. admissions officers and ESL teachers to become familiar with the range of tests produced in, or in collaboration with, the United Kingdom. It is hoped that this increased exposure to international use and interpretation will be accompanied by an increased recognition among examination boards of the need to validate their tests in ways that are considered internationally respectable and usual, and to present such evidence for the scrutiny of the public and of test users. Such efforts can only benefit the international community of test users.

6
ESL Composition Testing
Jane Hughey

Colleges and universities admit and place international students based on a variety of criteria, among which are students' academic records and their intended fields of study. However, since facility with language plays a large part in a student's ability to succeed academically, tests of English language competency are also of prime consideration in these decisions. This chapter focuses on the standards and expectations used to develop ESL writing tests, their construction and administration, what we can deduce from their results, and the kinds of tests that exist.

Academic Writing Standards and Expectations

In a recent survey of college and university faculty in a variety of fields (Bridgeman and Carlson 1983), respondents were asked, among other things, "Do you use the same standards for evaluating the writing of native and non-native speakers of English?" Results showed that a majority of the departments (69 percent) reported that they use the same standards to evaluate the writing of both native and non-native speakers of English. If most non-native students are evaluated by the same standards as native students, what then are the recognized standards for competence in writing for native speakers? Even though standards differ somewhat from one institution to another, a body of research identifies basic academic writing standards rather clearly.

For native speakers, college-level proficiency tests measure the kinds of academic writing required in most college courses; that is, to explain, defend a point of view, report facts and draw conclusions, or analyze and summarize passages—primarily expository writing (Ruth and Murphy 1988).

While there is a clear distinction between the academic skills needed by graduate and undergraduate students—some relating to skills specific to major fields (Ostler 1980)—and while different disciplines do not uniformly agree on writing demands or on a single mode of discourse for evaluating entering undergraduate and graduate students (Bridgeman and Carlson 1983), most researchers of both native and non-native students agree that basic academic requirements for beginning-level ESL students or advanced graduate students include the ability to produce various forms of writing, particularly expository and persuasive writing. Thus, it follows that "direct" writing tests should be constructed with these criteria in mind in order to identify writing strengths and weaknesses in the placement process.

Direct vs. Indirect Measures of Writing: A Rationale for a Direct Test of Writing

Currently, both indirect and direct tests of writing are available. Indirect tests—those most commonly used over the years to assess writing—measure examinees' recognition of correct usage in sentence-level constructions, spelling, and punctuation. Direct tests, on the other hand, require students to produce an actual composition. They test examinees' ability to communicate effectively: to develop content, organize ideas, and use appropriate vocabulary and syntax to express their ideas.

Those favoring indirect tests argue that "standardized or locally developed objective tests which measure a student's proficiency at choosing the best sentence or recognizing correct usage are . . . readily available and can be scored easily, efficiently and reliably. Moreover, scores from these tests of sentence structure, word choice, and style tend to correlate substantially with scores from tests based on actual samples of student writing" (Jacobs et al. 1981, 3).

In contrast, as Ruth and Murphy (1988) maintain, ". . . if writing is conceived of as a loose aggregation of skills, we may be satisfied with discrete-point, multiple-choice measures; however, if writing is conceived of as a complex, purposeful, cognitive act, we must demand writing tasks that draw on these communicative and cognitive processes" (p. 110). Since the first and most basic goal of any language test is to provide useful information about a learner's ability to communicate, a direct test of writing is desirable.

The Construction of Direct Tests of Writing

Writing tasks must be as reliable and as valid as possible. In other words, we must look carefully at (1) what the test asks examinees to do; (2) how we evaluate responses—in terms of evaluation criteria, reader qualifications, reader reliability, and reading situation; and (3) how we use the results. Users of the test—admissions officers or committees, program directors or coordinators—need to be familiar with the tests they are using. They should know how the tests are constructed, what the results will show, what significance the information carries, and whether the results meet their academic purposes for testing. Therefore, users also need to examine their purposes before making decisions based on the test results, since these decisions or actions are almost always of considerable consequence to their institutions or programs and to the students being tested.

If the purpose is to make admissions decisions, then a large-scale, standardized, holistically scored writing test, such as the TOEFL Test of Written English (TWE), or the Michigan English Language Assessment Battery (MELAB) Composition, provides a rough idea of an examinee's overall academic writing ability and probably yields, coupled with other scores, sufficient information for most, including borderline, admissions decisions. If the purpose is to make placement or instructional decisions, then locally administered or on-campus tests that yield specific information from a more diagnostic (analytical) scoring of the writing sample is preferable. All participants in the testing process should clearly understand the aims of the test so that the results can effectively serve the purposes for which they are intended.

Existing Composition Tests

The Michigan English Language Assessment Battery (MELAB). According to the test brochure (ELI 1989), the MELAB is designed to measure the English language proficiency of adult non-native speakers of English who will need to use the language for academic purposes at the university level. It is specifically designed to measure proficiency at advanced levels, and thus is not appropriate for beginning and lower intermediate students of English. The productive writing portion of the test purports to measure an examinee's ability to write with clarity, fluency, and accuracy in English. (See Chapter Three for a discussion of the rest of the MELAB.)

The direct writing test is administered as an integral part of the total MELAB. The test is started and stopped at specific times. Only official examiners administer the test, and test center personnel distribute and monitor it. At the conclusion of the test, papers are collected, kept secure, and sent to the English Language Institute at the University of Michigan (ELI-UM) for scoring. At the test, compositions are identified by the examinee's name, but identification codes are added to compositions after they arrive at ELI. Only the ELI-UM scores the MELAB and reports official MELAB results.

The writing test consists of a thirty-minute impromptu essay on an assigned topic, or prompt. Two prompts are given, and examinees may choose the one on which they prefer to write. The content of prompts ranges from topics requiring personal narrative to controversial issues requiring the examinee to take a position. Samples of MELAB test prompts include the following:

Would you raise your children the same way your parents raised you? Why? Why not?
or

If there were a country which was the single source of a major resource, would that country have the right not to share the resource with other countries? Why? Why not?

or

How should students be evaluated—according to their performance or their effort? Discuss.

Prompts such as these are developed by the ELI-UM research staff and are pretested using local international student populations. Prompts are kept secure; examinees have no prior access to the specific prompts that will be used on the test. However, prompts may be reused with different test populations. Sample lists of test topics are available to teachers and students for test preparation.

Scoring the MELAB Compositions. The MELAB final score is the average of the three parts of the test battery: composition, listening, and an objective test (grammar, cloze, vocabulary, and reading). The composition score range is from 53 to 97.

Compositions are read and scored at ELI-UM by a small, close-knit group of University of Michigan evaluators: test researchers and faculty who have undergone at least 20 hours of MELAB composition evaluator training, including background reading, criteria discussion, practice, and calibration with sample or "anchor" papers. (Scorers attempt to give the same score to the same composition independently.) Because the MELAB is administered frequently, evaluators score examinations continuously in small quantities. This may contribute to relatively high reliability: interrater reliability (the tendency for different raters to give a composition the same score) is between .85 and .92, and intrarater reliability (the tendency for the same rater to give the same score to the same composition a second time) is between .88 and .92. These are quite good reliability figures. (See Chapter Eight for a discussion of reliability.)

The compositions are scored holistically on what is effectively a ten-point categorical scale. In other words, the scorer reads the composition and gives it a single overall rating by assigning one of ten possible scores. The ten score categories are 53, 57, 63, 67, 73, 77, 83, 87, 93, and 97 (i.e., an evaluator will give one of these scores, not, say, a 75 or an 89). Two evaluators independently assess each essay, and their scores are averaged. A third evaluator, who may be any one of the trained evaluators, reassesses papers in one of two instances: when the two scores on a given paper differ by two or more categories (e.g., "73" versus "83") or in borderline cases when the average of the two scores changes the total MELAB score to a different recommendation category (e.g., a total score of 79 carries a different recommendation for academic work than does a total score of 80).

Using the Results. "Cut-off" scores, their interpretation, and recommendations for admission and placement are provided in the MELAB score report;

however, recommendations are based on UM standards, a factor that should be taken into consideration by other institutions using the test results. Even at UM, there are variations in the standards, depending on the applicant's field of study or department (e.g., higher proficiency levels are suggested in fields with a heavy reading load, such as history; slightly lower levels may be appropriate in fields such as mathematics). Furthermore, higher standards are suggested for undergraduates than for graduates, on the argument that slightly lower overall English proficiency will be compensated for among graduate students by their greater subject-area knowledge. Since 1989 the test results have included a diagnostic coding scheme whereby rhetorical, syntactic, and lexical features (positive and negative) noted by both readers will be reported as comments accompanying the numerical score. For example, a "97" paper is described as follows:

> Topic is richly and fully developed. Flexible use of a wide range of syntactic (sentence level) structures, accurate morphological (word form) control. Organization is appropriate and effective, and there is excellent control of connection. There is a wide range of appropriately used vocabulary. Spelling and punctuation appear error free. (ELI 1989, 13)

In addition to the numerical score and its interpretation, the report may contain one or more of 24 possible "letter codes" that provide diagnostic information to the examinee and to admissions officers or English instructors. These codes point out especially good or especially poor performance in the areas referred to in the description above (i.e., topic development, syntax, morphology, organization, connection, vocabulary, spelling, and punctuation).

Although results are usually available to the applicant and to specified institutions within two weeks following receipt of test papers, total turnaround time from initial application to score reporting is about six weeks.

The Test of English as a Foreign Language (TOEFL): Test of Written English (TWE). The TOEFL/TWE is offered by Educational Testing Service (ETS). Unlike the MELAB, the TOEFL did not include a direct writing sample prior to 1986. In the summer of 1986, after an extensive research and development effort, the TWE was administered as an experimental test, and since that time it has been available to candidates in several of the twelve official administrations each year. Since 1988-89 the TWE has been included in four yearly administrations: September, October, March, and May. At those TOEFL administrations that include the TWE, examinees write a short essay as a part of their total examination. The stated purpose of the TWE, according to the TWE Guide (ETS 1989), is to give examinees an opportunity to demonstrate their ability to communicate in English: to organize ideas on paper, to support those ideas with examples and evidence, and to compose in standard written English.

Administration of the Test. The TWE is administered only at official TOEFL testing centers and only by official TOEFL examiners. Examinees register for the test prior to its administration, go to a designated test center on a specified date, are admitted to the test only with appropriate identification (including photographs), and may not leave the testing site until the test has been completed. No one else is allowed in or out of the test site during the examination. Tests are started and stopped at specific times. Test center personnel distribute and monitor the test. Examinees' test papers are coded numerically to protect against bias that might result from personal information, such as name or nationality. After the test has been administered, papers are taken up, kept secure, and sent to Educational Testing Service for scoring.

Unlike the MELAB composition, there is no choice of topics on the TWE. The test presents a single prompt along with directions for taking the test. It requires candidates to write a thirty-minute impromptu composition on the assigned topic. The topic, or prompt, may require the examinee to express and support an opinion, choose and defend a point of view, or interpret information presented in a chart or graph (ETS 1989), but allows examinees to draw on their own experiences in responding. Examples of the types of prompt used for the TWE, taken from the TOEFL Test of Written English Guide (ETS 1989), appear below.

Example 1
   Traditional ways of life are often changed by modern technology. Using one or two examples of such changes, compare the new ways with the old. Which way of life do you like better? Why?

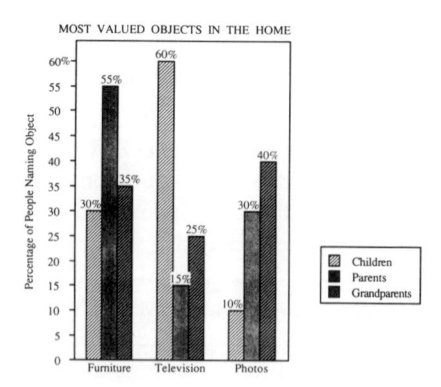

MOST VALUED OBJECTS IN THE HOME

[Bar graph showing Percentage of People Naming Object for Children, Parents, Grandparents across Furniture, Television, Photos:
- Furniture: Children 30%, Parents 55%, Grandparents 35%
- Television: Parents 60%, Grandparents 25%, Children 15%
- Photos: Children 10%, Parents 30%, Grandparents 40%]

Example 2
   This graph shows some people's responses to the question, "what objects in your home do you value the most?" Using the information in the graph, compare the value that different age groups place on different objects. Explain your conclusions, supporting them with details from the graph.

Different prompts are developed for each test administration by writing specialists from the United States and Canada and are reviewed and finalized by the ETS test development staff. Trial tests of the prompts are administered to various non-native English-speaking populations both in North American schools and in other parts of the world. Prompts for the TWE are secure; that is, examinees have no access to them prior to the test.

Scoring the TWE. Reading and scoring of the TWE is also standardized. All papers from an administration are read in regional locations in the United States and Canada during a two-to-three-day group reading. Qualified readers from all parts of the United States and Canada participate. Like the readers for the Michigan test, TWE readers are teachers with backgrounds in English or writing who have undergone training with the evaluation criteria, and have practiced with "anchor" papers for calibration. Throughout the evaluation session, readers recalibrate with additional sample papers while "table leaders," or supervisors, check periodically to ensure that readers are applying the criteria accurately and consistently in their assessments. Reading is holistic and rapid, approximately one to two minutes per paper, and the number of compositions read in any one assessment may range from 10,000 to 50,000 papers. With the TWE, interrater reliability is calculated after every administration, and ranges from .85 to .88, which is quite good.

The test is scored holistically on a six-point criterion-referenced scale (i.e., a scale specifying performance characteristics at each level) that identifies desirable qualities of writing, including organization, development, addressing the task, use of supporting details, unity, coherence, facility with the language, syntactic variety, and appropriateness of word choice. For example, the scoring guidelines (ETS 1986) describe a paper at level six as follows:

Clearly demonstrates competence in writing on both rhetorical and syntactic levels, though it may have occasional errors.

A paper in this category

- is well organized and well developed
- effectively addresses the writing task
- uses appropriate details to support a thesis or illustrate ideas
- shows unity, coherence and progression
- displays consistent facility in the use of language
- demonstrates syntactic variety and appropriate word choice

Using the six-point scale, two readers rate each composition independently, with a third reader, who may be the chief reader or a table leader, resolving discrepancies of more than one point (e.g., "1" versus "3").

Using the Results. A single TWE score (the average of the two readers' scores) appears on the TOEFL score report separately from the TOEFL score. No commentary is added as to the writer's performance, and no "cut off" scores or other recommendations are made to institutions based on the test results; however, the criteria and sample papers are available in the TOEFL Test of Written English Guide (ETS 1989) to guide admissions officers and program directors in decision making. Papers from each administration that includes the TWE are read within a few weeks after the test is administered, and test results are returned to candidates and specified institutions within four to twelve weeks after the scoring. Results, to date, appear to be used chiefly for admissions.

Since the test is designed for students at all levels, and since requirements and standards vary from one school to another and from one department to another, the significance of results will vary depending on the requirements of individual institutions.

Observations and Conclusions. Direct writing tests, vital indicators of students' academic performance and success, are commercially available in two somewhat different forms. With the MELAB, examinees choose to write on one of two topics, the design of which sometimes elicits personal narrative and sometimes reactions to controversial issues. With the TWE, examinees write on the one assigned topic, which is basically expository-persuasive in construction. Both tests are samples of first-draft writing taken in a brief time period. From the TWE, institutions receive a whole score that provides a rough idea about how students should be placed and information for admissions decisions. From the MELAB, somewhat more detailed information is available. These direct measures meet validity criteria (i.e., they have been shown to be related to students' abilities to write in actual academic situations), and their results reflect high reliability; therefore, it is safe to assume that the results give a fairly accurate indication of an examinee's capabilities in writing. However, in determining how to use the information available, Lloyd-Jones (1982) cautions that tests must be interpreted in light of their limitations.

Possible Limitations. While large-scale test results facilitate admissions and placement decisions for many institutions, there are occasional drawbacks. Large-scale tests are just that; they are administered to large numbers of students. As a result, test prompts are broadly designed to be accessible to all examinees at all language levels and, thus, do not necessarily elicit what would be termed "real writing"; that is, they are generally designed to reflect the following features:

- They allow examinees to address topics from personal knowledge, or with enough surface information that they may use that information to elaborate sufficiently on the topic.

- They can be addressed within an allotted, but brief, test time.
- They contain simple vocabulary so as to avoid misunderstanding or misinterpretation of the prompt (prompts that use extended reading passages run the risk of confounding examinees' reading and writing skills).
- They avoid topics that might trigger highly emotional, religious, or political responses that can and do affect performance.
- They represent first-draft writing.

Designed as they are, standardized, large-scale writing tests do not measure what a student might be able to write in English with more time or with editorial assistance, or in a different setting with a different topic and a different purpose. Rough assessments or whole single scores, such as the six-point scale, usually provide sufficient information for entrance or admissions decisions. This kind of score, however, often does not provide the kind of diagnostic information needed for effective placement, since little specific information about the various aspects of a candidate's writing ability is revealed. For example, a score of "4" may indicate weakness in use of vocabulary or sentence structures, but that same score may mean instead that the development of ideas and organization is weak. One "4" candidate may need only a grammar course or writing lab instruction, while another "4" would benefit from a full course in the principles of composition. These differences could also determine placement into full or partial schedules of coursework, depending on the student's field of study, the amount of writing required, and the departmental expectations for performance. Thus, a diagnostic-type, on-campus composition assessment is often more helpful than the TWE scale in making placement decisions.

Timeliness, or recency, of the test information is also an important factor. "Because language skills can change dramatically in a relatively short period of time, testing students in the United States some months after they took the TOEFL in their native countries might lead to inexplicable, confounding, and uninterpretable results" (Carlson et al. 1985, 5). Lag time between the test administration and the arrival of results at a designated institution can mean that the information is out of date. Since most schools set specific deadlines for admissions applications, time lags in reporting test scores may conceivably delay a student's enrollment by a semester or more. Consider also the case of students who do not request that their scores be sent to a designated school until sometime after taking the test. For instance, ETS considers TOEFL scores obsolete and does not report them more than two years after the time an examinee has been tested; nevertheless, two years is a considerable amount of time in terms of language development. Consequently, lag time may significantly affect important institutional decisions. If the institution relies on the accuracy of the results to indicate a student's writing ability for either essential or borderline admissions or for placement, by the time the student is admitted, the proficiency level may have changed significantly. First, students who have continued to develop their language skills between the time of the test and their admission to the school may be far better prepared to meet academic requirements than they were at the time of the test. Yet, with decisions based on their large-scale test scores, they could perhaps be excluded from some specific courses or from a full courseload. On the other hand, those candidates without a strong writing background who memorized "canned" topics or "crammed" for the test in order to achieve high scores will probably not be able to perform to that standard on a regular basis—unless in the interim they too have continued their language development. As a result, for delayed or borderline scores, in particular, local on-campus retesting is often advisable.

Consider, too, that those who simply had a bad test day may be more able to meet demands than they were at the time of the test, that one writing sample is not always an accurate representation of true skill, and that the test construction may have been weak or not in accord with the standards and expectations of a particular institution.

On Campus: Direct Tests of Writing

Direct tests of writing are also conducted as separate on-campus tests in many colleges and universities. A recent survey (see appendix B) of schools representing various geographic areas was conducted to determine whether and how local direct writing tests are being used. Information was gathered from the University of Toronto, Rutgers at New Brunswick, University of Michigan, Ohio State University, Colorado State University, University of Arizona, California State University at Dominguez Hills, Texas A&M University, Georgia State University, and Florida State University. The tests being administered in these schools bear a close resemblance to the large-scale tests; there are, however, some significant differences. Some of the following information, taken from the survey, may be of value to institutions implementing on-campus direct writing tests.

Local or on-campus direct tests of writing have developed, in most cases, because scores from the MELAB and the TOEFL, which many schools require applicants to submit for admissions, do not provide enough information for accurate placement into ability levels or specific classes with regards to writing. Consequently, a number of schools now use modified large-scale tests supplemented by their own on-campus writing tests, especially for placement purposes.

While the locally developed tests from most institutions are generally used as supplemental tests to the TOEFL or the MELAB, two academic institutions are mentioned separately here, since they both are developing comprehensive language testing. The University of Toronto, which accepts the MELAB, the TOEFL, or the British ELTS for admissions, has recently developed its own comprehensive test battery, the Certificate of Proficiency in English (COPE), consisting of listening, reading, speaking, and writing segments, as an alternative to the two standardized tests. The COPE, required for graduate students and with anticipated requirement for undergraduates within a year, is used for admissions, placement, and exit decisions. As an exit test, it serves as a seal of approval for the student's work. An applicant for admission may substitute the COPE test for the large-scale tests since it, too, is a comprehensive test. The four test segments are closely interrelated, and information from one segment is used as a basis for response in other segments. Rutgers, currently using one of the large-scale tests for admissions, is also in the process of developing its own comprehensive on-campus test that includes writing, reading, vocabulary, aural, and oral sections. Information about the COPE and Rutger's writing tests will also be included in the following discussion pertaining to all universities surveyed.

Administration of On-Campus Writing Tests. Unlike large-scale tests, on-campus writing tests are administered either during the first week of academic work or from one week to a few days prior to the quarter, trimester, or semester's work; consequently, they elicit up-to-date information about a student's writing ability. A number of schools also administer the writing tests as exit tests at the end of the study period to students who are placed in additional writing courses. Thus, the number of times the test is given during the year depends upon the local entrance, placement, and exit policies.

All schools surveyed, with the exception of Ohio State, which administers its direct writing test separately from other tests, give the test as part of a battery of on-campus tests, usually in conjunction with commercially available subcomponents of the MELAB or an Institutional TOEFL. Many schools administer the writing portion of the test as the first segment in the battery. However, at Florida State, the writing portion comes in the middle of the test; at Georgia State, the writing section follows and is based on the listening section of the test; at Rutgers, the writing test is based on a one- to two-paragraph reading section; and at the University of Toronto, the writing follows and is related to the reading and listening sections. In programs where the test is incorporated into a battery, the overall testing time ranges from two to three hours, with the writing portion ranging from thirty minutes to an hour.

The development of test topics varies from campus to campus. While California prompts are written, pretested, and refined by a statewide test development committee, prompts at Michigan and Texas A&M are developed by local test development staff; at other schools, prompts are developed by writing faculty members. Some schools field test their writing topics and others do not. Those who do not base their topic choices on past experience as to what works, while those who do field test do so on either current or previous small groups of foreign students within their local programs. In all cases, prompts are kept secure until the test is administered.

Four of the schools—Ohio State, Michigan, Georgia State, and Colorado State—give students a choice of topics on which to write, while Rutgers gives a choice of questions based on the reading selection; the rest of the schools surveyed offer only one prompt. Texas A&M, however, prepares one prompt for graduate students, which requires examinees to compose using the higher cognitive skills such as evaluation, hypothesis, projection, or persuasion; and a separate, less complex, one for undergraduates, which, for example, requires them to describe a process or compare familiar objects or situations.

As previously mentioned, Rutgers and Toronto use readings as the stimulus for the written essays, and Georgia State uses information from the listening section. Michigan prompts, derived from subject-specific material, include areas of interest such as the following:

> Explain what is meant by the term "computer languages." What further developments in this area do you expect to see in the next five years?
> or
> It is sometimes suggested that the Arts are becoming more "international," in other words, local cultural influences are declining. To what extent do you consider this to be true in any one art known to you (film, theatre, the novel, painting, etc.)?

Arizona prompts include a statement on a general topic such as pollution or technology, followed by a choice of two or three sentences, one of which examinees must choose to develop in their essay. The prompt below is one example. Students are instructed to begin the essay by copying the following sentence into their blue books:

> The level of compulsory education varies greatly from country to country.

They are then instructed to select one of the following sentences as their second sentence and copy it into the blue book.

1. Governments should reduce expenditures in other areas to guarantee that all citizens attain as much education as possible.
2. Although governmental support for education is important, often a country has more vital needs that must be met.
3. In some countries, a high level of education for all citizens is not necessary.

Students are instructed to complete the essay, developing the ideas that follow from the first two sentences.

As a result of the diverse populations and situations, prompts vary in basic design from those based on personal experience to controversial issues to subject-oriented topics; but most—Ohio State, Arizona, California State, Colorado State, Texas A&M, Florida State, and Rutgers—generally use briefly worded topics that elicit expository or persuasive responses calling for the writer to agree, disagree, or take a position with regard to the topic and allowing students to use experience-based examples in their responses.

Scoring the Tests. In addition to a felt need for production tests, some of the universities also expressed a need for more information from scores, and a number of the on-campus writing tests include a more in-depth analysis of students' productive writing skills. Texas A&M University, for example, uses a holistic/analytic scoring system based on a 100-point scale. Assessments are made of students' writing in five areas—content, organization, vocabulary, language use, and mechanics—and five component scores as well as a whole score are reported. A recommendation scale for placement within the university and within a regular or an intensive English program is keyed to the writing scores. The University of Toronto and Florida State University have also based their scoring and reporting on the Texas A&M model. The University of Michigan uses the ten-point scale described earlier, with commentary that provides specific information about student performance in rhetoric, syntax, and lexis and recommendations for placement into specific courses; Georgia State and Rutgers both use a six-point analytical grid that indicates performance in rhetorical development as well as in grammar and mechanics and includes specific recommendations based on the scoring information; and Ohio State publishes a writing course description that clearly indicates appropriate placement based on writing scores. The other schools in the survey use scoring criteria based on single whole scores ranging from four to six points, much like those used for the TWE.

On various campuses, readers for the tests may be curriculum supervisors, test administrators or developers, full- or part-time ESL and English faculty, or graduate students—all of whom are experienced in writing, writing research, or teaching writing. Most institutions, but not all, train their readers using some combination of testing manuals, scoring criteria, and sample papers. All schools, except Georgia State and Rutgers, conduct supervised readings in which raters meet together in a specific location at a specific time for the composition scoring. At Rutgers, the initial reading is done independently, yet the second readings and resolutions are conducted in group situations.

While Toronto sometimes uses one reader and Florida State uses three readers for each writing sample, the other testing programs use two readers, with a third reader only when there is disagreement equivalent to two points or more on a six- to ten- point scale. Third readers, in some cases, are selected randomly from among the reading group, except at Colorado State, California State, Rutgers, and Texas A&M, where chief readers usually resolve discrepancies. Rutgers and Texas A&M both give each paper two readings—one holistic reading for content and organization and the second for analysis of structure and mechanics.

Performance Factors

A number of psychological, cultural, and educational factors can affect examinees' performance on direct measures of writing as well as on other types of tests. While there is, perhaps, no way to eliminate the negative effects of test-taking, it is wise to consider these effects when making decisions based on test results. In *Learning Across Cultures,* Dunnet, with Dubin and Lezberg (1981), points out that "students arriving in the United States may hope that they will be required to learn only as much English as is needed to study their major field . . ." (p. 55), a fact particularly true for those who will study and then return home. When students apply to and enter American schools with this notion, their concept of how much English is sufficient may not coincide with what the academic institution thinks is sufficient. In this case, students' attitudes toward the language test can be a definite psychological factor in their success or failure on the test and also in their reactions to the test results.

On both large-scale and on-campus tests, cultural factors in educational background with regard to writing may also influence performance. For example, some test makers assume that "topics allowing students to draw on personal experience provide a better means of assessing general writing competency. However, . . . teachers of speakers of English as a second language report special problems with personal experience topics" (Ruth and Murphy 1988, 255). In fact, ESL students have difficulty with assignments that require that they reveal self and personality, such as personal letters. Their personal writing is often "little more than a stringing together of items with much emphasis on feeling and little on logic" (R. V. White 1980, 15).

Other factors that affect students' performance on or attitude toward the writing test and its results may include:

- Disorientation caused by jet lag or culture shock that the student is experiencing at the time of the test administration. This is especially true with on-campus tests.
- Fear of the test, or test insecurity. The educational systems in some other cultures do not include writing as a primary part of the educational experience; therefore, students from such backgrounds, having no idea of what is expected of them, may approach the test with fear and uncertainty. This anxiety may cause undue stress for the candidate and may result in attempts to "cram" for the test or even use stand-ins or "canned" (memorized) responses.
- Extreme worry or anger over test results when admission or placement involves additional unexpected coursework, costing students extra time and money.
- Professional embarrassment as a result of placement. For example, a student may be a graduate from an American university with one set of

standards and yet be required to enroll in additional intensive or other English courses in another university with different language requirements.

To guard against negative attitudes and reactions to test results, institutions should state clearly in all printed matter that goes out to foreign applicants (1) what the local standards, expectations, and testing practices are; (2) what large-scale and on-campus testing is required and when; (3) how test results will be used (i.e., the consequences or results of those tests); and (4) what the school's "cut" scores are, if any, for large-scale and also for on-campus tests. Publication of this information gives applicants an opportunity to prepare themselves for the test(s), and for the placement and the coursework they may anticipate based on the results.

A Checklist for Using Test Results

Since inaccurate admission or placement causes unnecessary problems for both students and academic institutions, admissions officers or program directors may want to consider several factors in their use of writing tests and writing test results:

- What kinds of decisions do you need to make? (Are test results to be used for admissions or for placement?)
- What kinds of information do you need in order to make your decision? What kinds of writing does your institution, or do your various departments, require of students?
- Based on these requirements, which kind of test provides the best information for your decision making: large-scale, on-campus, or both?
- Is the construction of the test prompt (e.g., personal, expository, persuasive, subject-specific) appropriate to test the kinds of writing your institution requires?
- Do the scoring criteria meet the standards and expectations for writing at your institution?
- Are you familiar with the significance of the scores? What exactly does a "3", "4" or "6", a "57", "63" or "87" represent?
- Based on the criteria, what "cut off" scores will you use to meet the admissions standards of your departments, college, or university?
- Is it important that you have the candidate's writing samples directly available to you?
- Does the candidate's field of study affect your decision? If so, how will the standards (scores) differ for various areas of study?
- Does the candidate's level of study—graduate or undergraduate—affect your decision? If so, what scores will you use in each case? If you administer an on-campus test, how will you distinguish between the performance of the two groups?

- Will the scores affect students receiving positions as graduate, teaching, research, or lab assistants?
- Does the recency of the scores affect your decision?
- Is the writing score considered by itself or is it averaged with other segments of a language test?
- Do you administer an on-campus direct writing test to help place students, or to clarify inconsistent or borderline admissions scores?

If scores are used for placement purposes, more factors need to be taken into account:

- What score(s) determine whether a student is automatically required to take additional writing classes?
- What kinds of courses are available: advanced placement English, regular or mainstream English, writing lab or basic English, grammar-based writing courses, intensive English or placement into levels within an intensive English program?
- What scores indicate placement into other academic coursework but with high, low, or no writing requirements?

Because direct writing tests are structured as they are, users need to be aware of their limitations, be familiar with the test construction and significance of results, use what is most appropriate to their particular needs, retest when results are questionable, and consider productive writing scores in conjunction with other indicators of the examinees' ability to use the language.

Conclusion

There is an obvious need to improve the quality of ESL/EFL writing in order to benefit both the foreign students entering our academic institutions and the institutions themselves. If we are consistent in our efforts to create and use appropriate tests, admissions and placements will be more accurate and more meaningful. If we are consistent in our testing, foreign students will seek to prepare well for direct measures of writing. They will come into our academic institutions better prepared to compete with English native-speaking students and succeed in their chosen fields of study. If what we test influences what we teach and what our students learn, the "backwash" effect of a direct measure of writing many improve many facets of ESL writing.

In summary, then, we may see the following as the advantages of a direct measure of writing ability:

- More valid than a discrete point test for providing information about communicative proficiency

- Easier to prepare than a discrete point test
- More "nearly certain to produce . . . meaningful and readily interpretable results" (Oller 1979, 229)
- More accurately indicates levels of proficiency and strengths and weaknesses in the composition skills
- Highly reliable if properly administered and evaluated
- Uses other participants (scorers) in the communicative process to judge the success or failure of the writer's communicative efforts
- Emphasizes the importance of language for communication
- Promotes a closer match between what is taught and what is tested

7
The Testing and Evaluation of International Teaching Assistants
Barbara S. Plakans and Roberta G. Abraham

Tests of non-native speakers' ability to communicate orally in a target language are qualitatively different from other kinds of language tests, as Underhill (1987) points out. They are time-consuming, expensive to administer, and difficult to score fairly. Only in the past decade has standard administration of tests of active speech production become the focus of widespread interest. The shift has occurred largely because of the urgent need at U.S. universities to test the speaking ability of large numbers of international teaching assistants (ITAs) to determine their fitness for classroom duties.

Unlike the numerous tests of reading, writing, and listening skills used to determine students' readiness for university study, oral testing has had a different impetus. Frequently this testing has been mandated by state legislatures, university governing boards, or university administrations to ensure that undergraduates taught by ITAs would be able to understand their accented English. Benefits to the ITAs of perfecting their speaking and presentation skills have been only a secondary concern.

The purpose of this chapter is to describe the types of tests now in use and their advantages and disadvantages. We will examine the Test of Spoken English (TSE) and its offshoot, the Speaking Proficiency English Assessment Kit (SPEAK); interviews, including the Interagency Language Roundtable/American Council on the Teaching of Foreign Languages (ILR/ACTFL) Oral Proficiency Interview (formerly known as the Foreign Service Institute Oral Interview); and several ITA performance tests developed by universities. We will then look briefly at issues that institutions should consider in setting up oral testing programs. We will begin, however, by considering the TOEFL, often used as an indirect measure of speaking proficiency.

Tests Used to Assess Speaking Proficiency: Their Advantages and Disadvantages

The TOEFL. The language test most widely used by U.S. universities for admission of international students is the Test of English as a Foreign Language (TOEFL), which was not designed as a measure of speaking proficiency but has been used indirectly as such on occasion. Some departments have hoped that setting a high TOEFL passing score would ensure that the foreign students they admitted had good English speaking ability. An Educational Testing Service (ETS) research study (Clark and Swinton 1979) mentioned that, on a group basis, a reasonably strong relationship seems to exist between skills measured by paper-and-pencil instruments such as the TOEFL and speaking proficiency as judged through the evaluation of speech production. They added that "for purposes of making highly reliable statements about the speaking proficiency level of individual test candidates, extrapolation on the basis of group correlational data may be considered a rather questionable procedure" (p. 1). This means that if, for example, individuals have had extensive training in grammar and reading, but not in speaking, their TOEFL overall scores may result in an overestimation of general proficiency based on those two skills.

Data collected over a four-year period at Iowa State University compared the most recent TOEFL scores of prospective ITAs with their scores on the SPEAK, a speaking test used by many universities to certify ITAs for teaching assignments (see discussion below). Most examinees with TOEFL scores over 600 received scores that permitted their placement in the classroom. However, SPEAK scores for examinees with TOEFL scores between 500 and 600, the range commonly used for admission to graduate programs (Johncock 1988), were distributed from very low to very high. Thus, it would be dangerous to rely on the TOEFL as a screening device for prospective ITAs with TOEFL scores below 600.

The TSE. Recognition of the need for a more direct, general purpose, practical speaking proficiency test led to the development of the Test of Spoken English (TSE) in 1980 (Stansfield and Ballard 1984). As outlined in Chapter Four, the TSE is administered by ETS at international TOEFL test centers five times per year and at designated testing centers in the United States four times per year on the same dates as the TOEFL. The test takes approximately 20 minutes and requires no writing, but instead uses examinee test booklets to provide instructions and cue examinees, and tape recorders to record their responses. The test has seven sections. Examinees have to answer biographical questions (not scored), read a passage aloud, complete sentences, tell a story based on a series of pictures in the test book, listen and respond to short-answer questions about another picture and to open-ended questions requiring either detailed description or expression of an opinion, and roleplay the presentation of an announcement to a class.

Examinee response tapes are forwarded to ETS, where they are rated independently by two trained raters. If the raters' scores do not agree, a third rater resolves the discrepancy between the two. Scores are sent to the examinee and to institutions specified by the examinee at the time of registration. Four separate test scores are reported: overall comprehensibility (on a scale of 0–300), and part scores for pronunciation, grammar, and fluency (each on a scale of 0–3). The overall comprehensibility rating is a global assessment, while the other three are diagnostic in nature and intended to offer analysis of a particular aspect of speech. A score of 0 is given for virtually no control, 1 for major errors that interfere with intelligibility, 2 for generally good control with some non-native errors, and 3 for intelligibility close to that of a native speaker. As with the TOEFL, ETS does not establish a passing or failing score; institutions requiring the test make this determination. In their survey of 34 universities, Riggles and Frampton (1988) found a range of minimum passing TSE scores of 220 to 250.

The TSE is designed to assess the ability to handle moderately complex language tasks and discriminates best at moderate proficiency levels of two and three on the ILR/ACTFL interview scale (discussed later in this chapter). Above those levels, a ceiling effect begins to appear (ETS 1982b). In other words, the TSE does not attempt to distinguish between near-native and highly proficient non-native speakers. In a validity study by Clark and Swinton (1980), the TSE overall comprehensibility score had a higher correlation with the ILR/ACTFL ratings (.79) than with the TOEFL (.57), confirming that the TSE is a better measure of speaking than of listening, grammar, or reading skills. Within the context of instruction at nine universities, Clark and Swinton found the TSE overall comprehensibility scores were more highly correlated with undergraduate students' evaluations of TAs' lecturing skills (.60) than with the more interactive skills of communication during office hours (.54), answering students' questions (.53), and understanding student questions (.52). TSE scores had only a correlation of .29 with overall teaching performance. This suggests that the TSE is a moderately good predictor of lecturing skills, less good at predicting one-on-one communication skills, and a rather weak predictor of overall teaching skills.

Advantages of the TSE. Testing costs the institution nothing, since examinees who are applying for admission to U.S. institutions pay ETS to administer and rate the test. (The current charge is $75 in U.S. currency, and will increase to $95 in 1990–91.) Using the TSE permits departments to offer teaching assistantships before graduate students arrive on campus with some assurance that their speaking proficiency is adequate to the task assigned. This preadmission decision avoids the problems and expense of having to deal with those with weak speaking skills, who may spend a semester or more in language classes and still not meet the university's minimum standards for ITAs. The TSE and the SPEAK have been praised for providing an "uncontaminated" speech sample. In other words, the problems associated with the presence of an interviewer are nullified (e.g., the interviewer changing questions from one examinee to the next, coaching the examinee, repeating or rephrasing the questions numerous times, or showing bias in favor of certain examinees).

Disadvantages. The lack of contamination mentioned above is also viewed as a weakness by some test administrators concerned with communicative competence. Examinees have frequently complained that the test is unnatural because examinees must speak to a machine and not to another human, are given only one chance to hear and respond to a task, are limited in response time, and are provided minimal context for the tasks they are asked to perform. This combination of factors leads to high test anxiety and may contribute to an examinee's poor performance. Some of the TSE/SPEAK tasks (e.g., completing sentences, telling a story with pictures) are not those that a TA would be called upon to perform. Listening skills, vital in a TA, are only marginally considered. The TSE is not designed to assess the examinees' teaching ability, command of their subject, or interpersonal skills in dealing with U.S. students—also important aspects of any TA's success. Because examinees are speaking directly into a microphone, raters cannot observe such weaknesses as speaking softly or making no eye contact with the listener. Also, since the time constraints do not permit a sample of extended discourse, the ITA's rapid delivery and/or non-American intonation and stress may not become evident.

Unless the most prestigious U.S. research universities require the TSE, other institutions will probably refrain from adopting it because the relatively high registration fee paid by the student could severely impede their international recruitment efforts.

The SPEAK. In 1983, ETS offered a retired form of the TSE to institutions who wished to administer and rate the test for local placement purposes. The Speaking Proficiency English Assessment Kit (SPEAK) with a training program for raters can be purchased for $300. There are three supplemental kits, each containing another form of the TSE, for $100 each. Kits contain materials to set up and administer a local testing program. They each include a guide, testing tape, reusable test booklets, and scoring sheets. ETS does not certify locally trained raters, and SPEAK scores cannot be used in lieu of TSE scores outside the institution that administered and rated the test.

Each institution must have facilities where the test can be administered, such as a language laboratory with general broadcasting facilities and headsets and tape recorders for each examinee. Raters must be recruited and trained using the ETS-designed training program, which requires approximately eight hours. They learn the criteria by practice-rating a series of tapes and then complete six test tapes to determine their reliability with ETS expert raters. Raters also need access to tape recorders to play back the tapes.

Advantages of the SPEAK. Since institutions own their test kits, the SPEAK can be administered at their convenience. The reputation of Educational Testing Service provides strong "face" validity for the test (i.e., to the layperson, the test appears to do what it purports to do), particularly among skeptical faculty from the sciences. The widespread adoption of the SPEAK by a number of schools provides a common index for the comparison of research studies. Transfer students occasionally request copies of their SPEAK results, which some institutions will accept in lieu of TSE scores.

The professional skill and resources of ETS were used to create the test tapes and instructions for administering the test. These materials are well prepared and easy to use. The rating scale of 0 to 3 is simple to learn and apply, and the program of rater training is well structured and easily carried out. The test is simple to administer, and ratings may be done afterwards at the convenience of the raters.

Disadvantages. Because of the reliance on recording equipment, technical difficulties may arise. Tape recorders may not record or recordings may have a disconcerting background noise that hinders raters' judgment. The average time for a rater to score each test is about 18 minutes, and two raters are always used. If a third rater is required to resolve a disagreement, the time for scoring a single tape may add up to nearly an hour. Time, personnel needed to administer testing sessions (30-40 minutes per administration), and the cost of audiocassette tapes make the test a time-consuming, labor-intensive, expensive proposition.

Barrett (1987) has cited other weaknesses (that apply as well to the TSE): He objects to the skill of reading aloud being rated for fluency, noting that many educated native speakers demonstrate poor fluency in such a task as well as in any other tasks that require thinking aloud. He believes that in the ETS training program there are inconsistencies in the ratings given to speakers exemplifying the various levels by the expert raters. For example, he believes one foreign accent seems to be valued more highly than others represented on the training tapes, thus leading to confusion and possible bias among new raters. No guidance is given raters on what constitutes a "good" answer; anything other than "I don't know" (an automatic zero) is rated, even if the examinee has misunderstood the question. Thus raters continually wonder how aberrant an answer has to be to receive a zero. Barrett was most disappointed in the lack of equivalence that he and others have perceived among the first three forms of the test.

Interviews

Interviews have been used for some time in evaluating oral proficiency. They can range from highly structured to very informal. Rating procedures likewise can vary widely. Several versions of this form of oral proficiency test are discussed below.

The ILR/ACTFL Interview. For three decades, the principal test for oral language proficiency was the interview developed by the U.S. Foreign Service Institute. It was adopted by other governmental agencies that needed to evaluate the foreign language speaking skills of diplomats, military personnel, Peace Corps volunteers, and others with overseas assignments. The federal agencies that have an interest in language teaching and assessment have formed the Interagency Language Roundtable (ILR), which, among other responsibilities, oversees the administration of the Oral Interview. The American Council on the Teaching of Foreign Languages (ACTFL) has recently adopted this interview procedure to assess oral proficiency in academic settings (ETS 1982a). In its present form, the interview is known as the ILR/ACTFL Oral Proficiency Interview. The interview consists of a face-to-face, tape-recorded conversation between an examinee and one or two trained interviewers, who rate the performance afterwards. For an advanced speaker such as an ITA, the interview would probably require 20 to 30 minutes. Ratings are expressed in global terms by comparing the totality of an examinee's speaking performance on a rating scale of 11 levels, including pluses and minuses, from 0 (no practical ability) to 5 (ability equivalent to that of an educated native speaker). Factors considered in rating the interview are pronunciation, fluency, grammar, and vocabulary, demonstrated in such tasks as answering and asking questions, narrating, and roleplaying.

Advantages of the ILR/ACTFL Interview. Interviews can be interesting to conduct and much less anxiety-producing for the examinees than the TSE/SPEAK. The interviewer's job is to find the highest level of speaking the examinee can sustain, looking for patterns of strength and weakness rather than specific errors. The oral interview provides a flexible context for observing general language ability. The content is tailored in large part to the interests and inclination of examinees in order to collect adequate samples of how well they can narrate and describe, ask questions, support opinions, hypothesize, and talk about unfamiliar topics. Other than the need for tape-recording equipment and a private room, the interview is easy to arrange.

Disadvantages. Some aspects of the ILR/ACTFL interview, however, make it impractical for use as an ITA screening instrument. Training for interviewer/raters is conducted by ETS, and ACTFL sponsors five or six week-long workshops held in various parts of the United States each year. Follow-up work is required for certification. The expense and time involved make it unlikely for a university to be able to certify the number of raters needed by a large screening program. Each pair of raters would be likely to interview no more than a dozen

ITAs per day, and even this number could be fatiguing because of the demands on the raters in tailoring the interview precisely to each interviewee's level of proficiency. Reliability among several pairs of raters who may be using different questions and tasks is also an area for concern. The BBE ("Big Brown Eyes") effect from conversing with an examinee with an appealing personality may lead to rater bias and contamination of the sample by inadvertent coaching from the interviewer. The examinee's control of an interview can interfere with the assessment. For example, a taciturn person may furnish monosyllabic responses too short to rate, while a loquacious person may make it difficult for the interviewer to manipulate topics sufficiently to probe for the speaker's highest level of proficiency. The ILR/ACTFL interview is primarily set in the context of a question-and-answer format, providing little opportunity to observe some of the other speaking situations and skills required of a successful ITA. These advantages and disadvantages frequently apply to other types of interviews described below.

Other Interviews. The classic version of the ILR/ACTFL type of interview is used as a TA screening device by at least five universities, according to a survey by Johncock (1988). Some variations of it are used by 30 out of 60 institutions in Johncock's study and 14 out of 34 institutions in the Riggles and Frampton survey (1988). Johncock provided the following summary of conductors of the interview (not specified in 12 cases):

Head of hiring department	8
English language center	4
Graduate school personnel	3
TA supervisor in hiring department	2
Other	1

In some cases these interviews were conducted long distance over the telephone by the hiring department. The logistics of setting up such calls and assurance that the prospective TA is the speaker at the other end of the phone are two problems with such arrangements.

Two universities that have reported success in conducting ITA interviews are Southern Illinois and Michigan State. Since 1974, Southern Illinois has used a tripartite interview format. Three faculty members serve as raters: a representative of the hiring department, an ESL faculty member, and an associate dean of the Graduate College. The test begins with students answering general information questions and discussing their reasons for choosing the university, their field of study, plans for the future, and prior teaching experience. The department representative poses a topic for the student to teach or explain at the blackboard, while the other raters serve as "students" and ask questions. After approximately 20 to 25 minutes, the candidate is excused from the room while the examiners rate the student independently using a five-point scale with three criteria: comprehension, pronunciation, and fluency. The examiners compare their ratings and, according to Carrell, Sarwark, and Plakans (1987), have no difficulty reaching a consensus.

In the fall of 1986, Michigan State University found that its oral interview correlated highly enough with the SPEAK for it to be able to drop the latter. The 20-minute interview has since been revised by Barrett (1988) to include such features as (1) a warm-up with introductions and general information-gathering; (2) a list of 20 technical terms from the examinee's academic field to be pronounced; (3) an explanation and/or discussion of an article from his/her own field with questions about it; (4) either a comparison of teaching practices in the student's home country with those in the United States or an office hour role-play in which the interviewer assumes the role of an undergraduate with a problem; and (5) a classroom announcement role-play. If the interviewee's performance on the first three sections is either very good or mostly unintelligible, interviewers may consider ending the oral interview and making a decision at that point. Interviews are conducted by experienced ESL staff members and recorded on audiotape. They are scored by two raters on a scale of 1 to 4 in the following areas: oral production (consisting of pronunciation, vocabulary use, grammar, and fluency); aural comprehension (consisting of question handling, appropriate responses to the interviewer's comments, and understanding instructions); and discourse strategies (consisting of organization and sensitivity to the interlocutor's needs for clarification, restatement, and emphasis).

Performance Testing

Opportunities for prospective teaching assistants to demonstrate their ability to communicate in the a classroom in their own field of study take the form of teaching simulations, mock teaching sessions, question-handling situations, and role-plays of classroom management and office hours. Despite the suggestion by Brown, Fishman, and Jones (1989) that such simulations are evaluations of teaching ability to which ITAs—but not U.S. TAs—are subjected, advocates of these tests would claim that their intent is to measure communication skills in a functional context. For over a decade second language proficiency specialists have considered performance tests an appropriate way to determine whether someone's English is sufficient for teaching (Jones 1979). Twenty-nine (45 percent) of the 64 universities included in Johncock's (1988) survey reported using a performance test. Riggles and Frampton (1988) found that 60 percent of the 34 institutions they surveyed employed either a performance test or an on-site evaluation of ITAs' teaching skills. Some of the variations of performance tests include the TEACH at Iowa State University (Abraham, Klein, and Plakans 1986), the mock teaching test at Ohio State University described by Sarwark (Carrell, Sarwark, and Plakans 1987), and the classroom management role-play and question-handling task as part of the test at the University of Michigan (Briggs 1986).

In the case of the TEACH test at Iowa State University, examinees register a day ahead and are given a topic from a list suggested by the department in which they expect to teach, a textbook in which the assigned topic appears, and instructions on how to prepare for the simulation. Testing takes place in a typical classroom and lasts ten minutes. Examinees are allowed a minute or two at the beginning to become familiar with the surroundings, to write key terms, diagrams, or formulae on the chalkboard and to meet the "class" (three students, two raters, a test proctor, and a technician, who videotapes the performance). They have five minutes to explain some aspect of the assigned topic clearly and in words that an undergraduate class could understand, followed by three minutes of questions by the students (generally science and engineering majors). Two raters, who are trained ESL or speech instructors, independently rate the examinees' presentations on the spot. The videotape is useful in various ways: if the raters do not reach a consensus, it can be rated again; for diagnostic purposes, it can be viewed by the instructors of the ITA training courses; for self-critiquing purposes, examinees can borrow the tape and look at themselves; and for comparative purposes at the end of ITA training courses, instructors and trainees can see the amount of improvement.

Raters score each performance using four categories: overall comprehensibility, consisting of pronunciation, grammar, and fluency (as in the TSE/SPEAK); awareness of appropriate teacher-student relationships in a U.S. university classroom setting; ability to understand and answer students' questions; and communication skills, such as explaining the topic clearly, using supporting evidence and/or examples, addressing the "class," using the chalkboard effectively, and showing interest in the subject and in the students as learners. A scale of 0 to 3 is used, also modeled on TSE/SPEAK criteria (0 = not competent, 1 = not adequate, 2 = minimally adequate, and 3 = competent).

At the Ohio State University, prospective ITAs with SPEAK scores falling between 200 and 230 have the option of taking a mock teaching test or taking one or two quarters of spoken English coursework. (Those with scores below 200 are automatically assigned to a spoken English course.) The mock teaching test is also used as the exit test for the upper-level spoken English course. This test, which is videotaped, consists of a 10- to 12-minute lesson that the ITA presents to a panel of three raters (an ESL staff member, a faculty member representing the ITA's department, and a faculty member from another department) who act as the students. Thirty minutes before the testing time, ITAs arrive at the preparation room and receive material consisting of a description sheet for a course in their major department and two basic topics taken from their field of study. They are instructed to divide their allotted ten- to twelve-minute presentation into an introduction, a brief discussion of the course description, and a five- to seven-minute lesson based on one of the two topics. The panel of raters asks questions throughout the presentation. Afterwards the panel assesses the performance and reaches a consensus about whether the ITA may be certified. If a consensus is not reached, the videotape is sent to a member of the ESL advisory board for the final decision.

Another approach is used by the University of Michigan (Briggs 1986). In addition to an oral interview and the presentation of a short lesson, ITAs are required to participate in a classroom management role-play and a question-handling task. Evaluators from the English Language Institute and from the ITAs' hiring departments are thus able to assess tasks representative of some important demands of the teaching role. Five role-play situations representative of routine classroom management duties (rescheduling class or office hours, making an administrative announcement, or discussing test results) are briefly described in writing to the examinee shortly before the test. The ITA is supposed to do whatever is prompted by the situational task, and the evaluators in the audience take on the role of students. As a matter of principle, only one evaluator knows which task the ITA is handling. The task provides evidence of the examinee's efficiency, appropriacy, and clarity in handling interactive duties.

A question-handling task in the Michigan evaluation involves the presentation on videotape of eight questions typical of those undergraduates might ask ("How much does homework count in our grade?" "If I'm having trouble with an assignment, when can I come and see you?"). Two Michigan students, native speakers of English, alternate as questioners on the videotape. The tape is stopped after each question for the ITA's response. Questions are generally presented only once, except that the first one may be repeated if the ITA desires it. The task takes about three minutes. Evaluators attend to whether examinees understand the questions and how well they respond.

Advantages of performance tests. As Byrd (1987) has pointed out, such performance tests have strong face validity with examinees, departments, and undergraduate students. They are direct and attempt to reveal both culture and communication problems. The examinee must interact with questioners, who are (or are acting like) students, providing a more realistic and communicative test than either the TSE/SPEAK or an interview. Examinees usually like to talk about their own discipline and to have a chance to prepare their comments before they present them. Raters frequently say that they prefer live testing so they can take into account examinees' discourse strategies and teacher presence, which sometimes compensate for other linguistic flaws. Having the rating done simultaneously with the testing makes it possible to certify and place ITAs rapidly instead of having to wait for raters to review tapes as is the case with the TSE/SPEAK. Having a videotape of the performance is also a useful record that can be used to justify decisions, diagnose problems, etc. Performance tests that include a representative of the hiring department involve these departments more closely in the process, make them aware of the ramifications of their admissions decisions, and ensure that the recommendations of the panel are followed. The presence of students as questioners also contributes to the face validity of the test.

Performance tests have had an unanticipated side effect: They have contributed to campus-wide discussions about the nature of good communication and effective teaching techniques and how these elements can be assessed— important issues of concern to both native and non-native speakers, from TAs to senior professors.

Disadvantages. Such tests can be expensive because of the videotaping and hiring of questioners. They are also time-consuming and difficult to administer, particularly since a number of students, faculty and/or administrators must be convened to listen to the performances. As Byrd (1987) points out, the simulation test is most likely a waste of time, energy, and funding for ITAs with low-level language skills. Because there is no standardized performance test sanctioned by ETS or another testing service, scores cannot be compared between institutions. Some aspects of a performance are difficult to quantify or even to evaluate in a short time (e.g., overall organization and use of examples). The involvement of questioners can "contaminate" the speech sample if they confuse, intimidate, or interrupt the examinee. Raters who have been given scoring sheets to use in evaluating performance tests have commented that (1) they found it difficult to attend to all the skills to be rated, and (2) sometimes they knew so little about the technical or scientific topics presented by the examinees that they could not tell whether the examinee had answered a student's question appropriately and/or had explained some concepts adequately. Raters normally become tired after two or three hours of performances and may lose their objectivity. Naturalness is also difficult to build into some simulations. While many TAs lecture in the manner prescribed by the test, some do not (e.g., TAs in chemistry laboratories or foreign language classrooms).

Test Batteries

Some universities use a battery of tests (two or more different tests, each looking at oral proficiency through its own particular window) to get a more complete picture of the examinees' strengths and weaknesses. For example, the SPEAK might be used with an oral interview and/or a performance test to determine who is eligible for assignment to the classroom.

Since current evidence does not point clearly to any one test as the most comprehensive, reliable, or valid (Constantinides 1987), the battery approach may be appropriate where resources permit.

Table 1 summarizes important features of the five types of tests described in this section.

TABLE 1
CHARACTERISTICS OF ITA TESTS

Characteristics	TOEFL	TSE	SPEAK	Interview	Performance
Assesses speaking proficiency	no	yes	yes	yes	yes
Assesses listening proficiency	yes	marginally	marginally	yes	usually
Assesses cultural awareness	no	no	no	yes	yes
Assesses teaching ability	no	marginally	marginally	possibly	yes
Expensive for examinee	no*	yes	no	no	no
Expensive for university	no	no	yes	moderately	yes
Easy to administer	n.a.	n.a.	moderately	yes	no
Easy to rate	n.a.	n.a.	yes	no	moderately
Requires complex equipment	no	yes	yes	no	usually
Requires rating training	n.a.	n.a.	yes	yes, extensively	yes
Produces anxiety in examinee	yes	yes	yes	moderately	yes
Produces standardized results	yes	yes	yes	no	no
Produces uncontaminated speech sample	n.a.	yes	yes	no	no

*Usually a required admission expense already

Needs and Resources to Consider in Setting Up a Program

The most suitable oral testing approach will be determined by the needs of the institution and the resources at its disposal. Among the major issues to be considered are the size of the undertaking, time constraints, and the use of test results. Availability and cost of resources—equipment, tapes, rooms for testing, trained raters to assess the tests, and a supervisor qualified to train raters, administer the test, and interpret the results—must also be taken into account.

The initial step in setting up a program is to decide which office will be responsible for it. Programs seem most effective if they are housed in, or at least strongly supported by, a branch of the central administration with the authority to require departments to comply with test results. ESL, English, speech, or instructional development departments may lack the "clout" necessary to do more than recommend departmental action. In all cases, however, the administrator of the ITA program must develop and nurture a working relationship with the departments who send potential ITAs for screening. The administrator should know what types of duties the departments assign TAs (whether they oversee laboratories, handle discussion sections, lecture, grade papers, or perform other duties unique to particular departments), who supervises TAs and serves as a faculty liaison when questions arise about ITAs, whether the department is supportive toward the ITA screening program, etc.

The next step concerns testing itself. A first question involves the purposes that the testing must serve. There are at least four possibilities: Is the test designed to measure the examinee's overall ability in speaking proficiency and to serve as an admissions test? Is it designed to diagnose strengths and weaknesses of the examinee? Will the test results be used to place unsuccessful examinees in specific speech or ESL courses? For the examinees who complete these courses, will the test measure improvement? The testing supervisor needs to determine the purpose before deciding which tests will be needed. Another question concerns whose perception of English proficiency should determine the passing score—ESL expert raters (skilled in linguistics, but also in understanding foreign accents), faculty members from the hiring departments, undergraduate students, and/or college administrators.

The usual psychometric issues must also be considered: What sort of reliability and validity do the tests under consideration have? At what ability level do they discriminate best? The scale for the original ILR oral proficiency interview, for example, is designed to measure the highly proficient speakers in five high levels (3, 3+, 4, 4+, and 5), while the ACTFL/ETS derivative scale lumps highly proficient speakers into one level (Superior) and breaks up the low end of the ILR scale from three levels (0, 1, and 1+) into seven (0, novice-low, novice-mid, novice-high, intermediate-low, intermediate-mid, and intermediate-high).

What sort of rating scale will the raters use? What criteria will the raters be judging? What experience should the raters have and how will they be trained to do the rating? How will their reliability be monitored? What will be used as a passing score? Assuming two raters are used to assess each examinee, how much of a discrepancy between raters' scores will be allowed before a third rater is used? How and to whom will the test results be reported? How will test security be handled, particular if only one version of the test exists? How will ITAs who have not yet arrived on campus be informed about reporting to take the test? Will there be a mechanism for decreasing their anxiety by providing them with directions and sample questions beforehand?

In planning a screening program, it is important to consider the impression it will create. The ITA issue has become the source of much complaining by students, their parents, and others disturbed by the lack of concern some departments have shown in making teaching assignments and supervising ITAs. Administrators will point to the screening effort when they are approached with complaints. It is important that the program maintain high visibility and that someone be prepared to answer specific complaints. A system of record-keeping and evaluation should be set up from the beginning to provide evidence of success (see, for example, Abraham and Plakans 1988). Related issues, not germane to this chapter, include what is to be offered to ITAs who do not pass the screening. Can they retake the test, and if so, how soon? Is some training offered to them to help them improve their speaking/teaching skills? Another aspect involves trying to persuade undergraduates to be more considerate and helpful in dealing with ITAs (Smith 1988; vom Saal 1987).

As this chapter indicates, a great deal of work has been done in the past few years in ITA programing around the country to develop viable tests of oral proficiency. The result is a variety of screening measures that can be used, singly or in combination, to assess the skills of prospective ITAs. The future should hold more permutations of these measures as institutions adapt basic approaches to meet their individual needs.

8
Interpreting Test Scores
Grant Henning

Of central importance in the application of English language tests in colleges and universities is consideration of the precise meaning of the scores derived from these tests. This chapter is concerned, therefore, with issues related to appropriate interpretation of such test scores. Most of these issues may be grouped under two primary headings: *validity* issues and *reliability* issues. Most standardized language tests that are available for public use are accompanied by user manuals with information concerning test validity for given purposes and test reliability as measured in various settings by a variety of computational methods. Absence of such accompanying information imposes a burden on the test user and violates a tenet of good testing practice (Committee to Develop Standards 1985). However, even when such information is provided by the test developer, appropriate score interpretation in any given assessment context requires serious attention to issues set forth in this chapter.

The extent to which a given test measures the abilities or knowledge that it is purported to measure is an indication of the validity of that test. Tests may be valid for some purposes and not for others. The score interpreter must be concerned with not only what the test is *intended* to measure and whether it *accomplishes* its intended purpose, but also with whether the actual application and interpretation are *appropriate* to the intended purpose. The following validity concerns are related to score interpretation.

Test Validity Concerns for Score Interpretation

Population Appropriacy. Any user of a test should consider the population of examinees on which and for which the test was developed. Test scores must be interpreted not only with certain content or abilities in mind, but also in recognition of the targeted examinees. When tests are developed, items are selected or rejected on the basis of the way in which those items function when applied to the targeted examinees. This implies that qualitatively different kinds of tasks may be appropriate for qualitatively different kinds of examinees. For example, use of an adult ESL proficiency test to gauge language ability of native English-speaking children would likely produce scores that are uninterpretable, even though the mean scores for the two populations may be identical. Care should be taken to apply tests and interpret results only for the appropriate intended examinee populations.

Included here is the notion of test and item bias for groups of persons. If tests or items function differentially for subgroups of the targeted population, and if this results in scores that differ due to group membership of the examinees rather than due to differences in what is supposed to be measured by the test, then such tests or items may be biased. University admissions ESL tests that show significant score advantages for students in certain academic majors may be biased in favor of those majors owing to a disproportionate presence of familiar test content. The point relating to score interpretation is that the scores on such tests may not mean the same thing for persons in those advantaged majors as for persons outside of those majors. It is incumbent on the test developer and the test user to determine that significant extraneous biases are not present when the test is applied for the intended purposes.

Achievement/Proficiency Concerns. Some university admissions ESL tests (e.g., the Certificate of Proficiency in English and the First Certificate in English produced by the University of Cambridge Language Examinations Syndicate) are produced in conjunction with an instructional syllabus and may therefore be classified as *achievement tests*. Thus, scores on the examinations should reflect how well the examinees have mastered the content and skills that were taught them in the prior instructional sequence. Other ESL admissions tests, such as the Test of English as a Foreign Language (TOEFL) or the Michigan English Language Assessment Battery (MELAB), are purported to measure language proficiency independent of any particular instructional sequence and are thus *proficiency* tests. Even though some of the item types may appear quite similar for achievement oriented tests and proficiency oriented tests, the differences in ways in which examinees are identified and prepared and in the constraints on content selection suggest that the test scores may have quite different meanings. In such cases, extreme caution is warranted in any attempt to find score equivalencies across examinations. The expectation would be that any table of equivalencies would be highly dependent on the person samples and the test forms used in such a study, and may not generalize to other examinee samples or versions of the tests.

Criterion-Referencing and Norm-Referencing Concerns. Raw scores or even percentage-correct scores on a test really have no meaning until those scores are referenced to some standard. Most standardized ESL proficiency scores are primarily referenced to group performance. That is, "high score" or "low score" is defined by reference to the position of that score among scores attained by other examinees. To say that a person's performance was above average for the group is to assign meaning to the score on the basis of how others performed, which is called *norm-referencing*.

On the other hand, scores may be referenced to desired levels of attainment or mastery of content or skills rather than to the performance of groups of individuals. To report that a person attained a score of 4 on an Interagency Language Roundtable oral proficiency interview is to indicate that that person has demonstrated ability to use the language tested with a level of facility that corresponds to the performance descriptors associated with level 4, regardless of how other interviewees may have performed. Such tests are sometimes called *criterion-referenced* tests. The important point here is that the meaning of all test scores must be determined with reference to some standard. The persons interpreting the scores can only do so by considering the standards said to be referenced.

In practice, the distinctions between these kinds of standards may diminish when, for example, scores like 550 on the TOEFL or 85 on the MELAB are said by some academic admissions officers to constitute evidence that the examinee is qualified for admission to their institution insofar as English language ability is concerned. In such cases, external criteria have been established on the basis of experience to become the basis of score interpretation, and norm-referenced tests have, in one sense, become criterion-referenced on application. The challenge for the score interpreter is to determine whether standards chosen on such tests are valid indications of the levels and qualities of performance said to be required for the particular institution or educational purpose concerned. Again, reliance may be placed upon user manuals reporting the results of research to supply such information. It is not always the case, however, that such research has actually been conducted or that manuals are available.

True Score Drift and Shifting Standards. Language tests can be said to be designed to measure certain abilities within certain limits of accuracy. In this way, acknowledgement is made that there is always a degree—hopefully small—of quantifiable *measurement error*. The error-free portion of a person's performance on a test is sometimes called that person's *true score*. Important here is the consideration that true scores may change over time, quite apart from changes in test reliability or accuracy. Imagine a situation in which a reliable and valid ESL admissions test is developed, but following the publication of the test there is a major change in ESL curricula such that a sizable component of instruction in some parts of the world is either specifically aimed at preparing students to succeed with the ESL test in question or, conversely, is no longer related in any way to the content and skills tested. As a result, the mean score of test takers may shift upwards in some geographical regions and downwards in others. These kinds of true score drift can affect the meaning of test scores and can alter the utility of previously established admissions standards. Such drift would present problems in interpreting scores, since standards set in early administrations of the tests would not have the same meaning in subsequent administrations. Sometimes true score drift can be observed when sufficient numbers of equated forms have not been developed. In this case, drift may be the result of security breakdown. If tests have not been formally equated, and if admissions are based purely on selection of a set percentage of the highest scoring group of students each term, standards may shift at the institution as a function of shifts in the calibre of applicants. Admissions standards should be studied regularly at user institutions to determine whether those standards continue to be appropriate.

Dimensionality and Weighting Concerns. Often, university admissions ESL batteries are comprised of a variety of tasks purposely designed to measure different skills and abilities. This is a legitimate reflection of the intention for the test battery to be in some sense comprehensive. Test batteries may contain measures of reading comprehension, listening comprehension, writing ability, speaking ability, and grammatical accuracy, just to name a few possibilities. However, it is possible that the tasks required in the various subtests of the battery are so diverse as to constitute different domains or *dimensions of performance* in a statistical sense, and the test would be classified as *multidimensional*. When that happens, it is important that each unique component of the battery should have its own reported score.

Reporting one global total score for a multidimensional test raises serious questions about the appropriate weighting of each dimension and doubts about the validity of the test battery. It becomes difficult, if not impossible, to interpret global scores for a multidimensional test because the total scores are dependent on the weights given to the unique components. These may, in fact, not even be additive, in the sense of "trying to add apples and oranges." The score interpreter should first check to see if research evidence has been provided that the test is *unidimensional*, i.e., that it tests a single ability. If the test has been shown to be multidimensional, then individual scores should be reported, reflective of the ability said to be measured by each dimension.

Interpretation of Ratings of Language Performance. Tests of language production, whether oral or written, usually require use of qualified raters to serve as judges for the assignment of scores to the product. Involvement of raters, as opposed to the simple tallying of the number of correct items on an item-based test, poses certain problems for interpretation of scores. To understand what the ratings mean it becomes necessary to know what was in the mind of the rater at the time the ratings were assigned. As mentioned earlier, the rater may have simply been ranking performance in a norm-referenced sense. In this case, a high score would mean simply that the examinee performed better than other examinees in the judgment of the rater. Alternatively, the rater may have had some fixed standard of performance such as a rating schedule of performance criteria in mind, in which case a high score would signify that, in the judgment of the rater, the examinee exhibited the behavior associated with a high score. If the rating criteria were not explicit, or if rater compliance with the criteria were not verified, it would become extremely difficult to know what the ratings signified. Interpretation would require questioning the raters about their performance with each test rated. It is usually important to employ more than one independent rater and then check to see if the raters agreed in their ratings. While this procedure will not in itself guarantee that the meaning of the scores will be known, at least if there is a high degree of interrater agreement in scoring, then we have evidence that raters were attending to the same performance characteristics.

Appropriateness of Validity Evidence. No test is valid for every testing purpose. The test developer should indicate to users the purpose(s) for which the test was developed and provide evidence that the test is valid for the purpose(s) indicated. Awareness of the kind of validity evidence provided is highly important for correct score interpretation. University admissions ESL tests that offer only evidence of *concurrent validity*, i.e., high correlations with other university admissions tests, can inform the score interpreter only that the scores mean something similar to the scores of the other tests. This is really only informative if the meaning of the other test scores is known. So, concurrent validity evidence may not be sufficient by itself to inform score interpretation. Expert judgment of *content validity* for the intended measurement purpose is informative about the nature of the abilities measured. Thus, highly-rated content validity may indicate that all of the test content is relevant and appropriate. However, it does not inform the user whether a score of 50 is good or bad for some intended purpose. Evidence of *predictive validity*, i.e., how well success with the test signifies future success in some targeted endeavor, such as university studies, would be highly important in the case of university admissions ESL tests. Here caution is needed in the selection of the criterion of success. University grade-point average (GPA) may not be an appropriate or sufficient criterion for judging the predictive validity of ESL admissions tests. This is due in part to the varying demands for English language facility across institutions (e.g., trade schools, community colleges, or universities), majors (e.g., music, mathematics, chemistry, or linguistics), and course type (e.g., labs, lectures, or seminars). University academic counselors will recognize that it is not at all uncommon to find students in their final two years of undergraduate study at some institutions who have near 4.0 GPAs but may not have been able to satisfy their ESL requirements. This suggests that other criteria, such as subject-area faculty ratings of student ability to communicate in English, or employer satisfaction with communication skills, may be superior to GPA as criteria for predictive validity.

Test Reliability Concerns for Score Interpretation

Test reliability is related to the consistency and accuracy of the scores reported for a given test. Test scores should tend to rank-order the examinees in the same way on repeated administrations. There should be a tendency towards the widest possible variation in the range of obtained scores, rather than a score distribution in which all examinees tend to obtain similar scores and are therefore indistinguishable on the ability being measured. In order for interpretation of scores of university admissions ESL tests to be fair, reliability estimates above .90 on a scale of zero to one are usually warranted. These estimates should be available in the user manual accompanying the test. The following additional score interpretation concerns are also related to test reliability.

Measurement Error and Cut-Off Decisions. Highly reliable tests will have low measurement error and high accuracy by definition. Yet all tests have some expected measurement error that is usually reported as the *standard error of measurement* for those tests. When ESL admissions cut-off scores are set, such as 550 or 600 on the TOEFL, it is important to recognize that a small but constant amount of error exists in the estimation of ability at the decision point. Thus, a person with 547 may be fully qualified for admission, whereas it is equally possible that a person with a score of 553 obtained by fortuitous guessing may *not* be fully qualified. This suggests that, if available, other information can be useful at the cut-off point. For example, if it is known that the person who scored 547 was ill or otherwise incapacitated on the day of the examination, that information may lead the counselor to decide that the candidate be retested.

Also, it should be recognized that the farther the cut-off score is set away from the mean of the distribution, the smaller will be the degree of confidence that can be placed in the resultant decisions. In the case of the TOEFL there will be greater decision accuracy around the 500 point than around the 450 point, and greater accuracy around the 575 point than around the 625 point. However, institutions that are not prepared to offer compensatory English instruction may prefer the risk of erroneously rejecting some excellent candidates, by applying cut-off scores very strictly, to the risk of admitting some candidates who are inadequately prepared in English by allowing flexibility in cut-offs. (See Chapter Two for a pragmatic discussion of these issues from an admissions officer's point of view.)

Equated Forms. The science of developing equated forms of tests is well developed. Surprisingly, however, not all developers of university admissions ESL tests have bothered to equate the various versions of their tests statistically. In such cases, the score interpreter can never know for sure that a score obtained on one form of the test means the same as a score obtained on another form of the same test. In order to determine whether test forms have been statistically equated and, if so, by what method, the user of admissions tests should consult the user manuals provided or contact the user information service office. Potential score interpretation problems are not avoided by failure to produce equated forms of tests. Large-scale testing programs that do not provide alternate forms of tests are likely to experience early breakdowns in security, so that test scores will soon lose their value for decision-making purposes.

Test Administration Conditions. Some test developers offer versions of their tests for institutional use. Usually such test versions are released to the institution for private administration and possibly even scoring of the tests. In this way, test versions such as the Institutional TOEFL, MTELP, MTAC, and SPEAK are made available to institutions at a cost savings, but with no commitment that the scores on those tests will be accepted at other institutions for decision-making purposes. In order for such scores to be meaningful, it is necessary that the manner of administration conform to the manner followed with the original examination. The time allowed for testing, the sequencing of testing tasks, the quality of equipment used, and the monitoring or proctoring of the tests should all conform to the regulations followed for the noninstitutional versions of the tests if the test scores are to be interpreted in the same way. Slight changes in conditions of test administration can alter the meaning of test scores and make such scores difficult to interpret.

Retest Practice/Learning Effects. It is important to note that the meaning of test scores can change with practice opportunities. For this reason, permission to repeat some institutionally developed and administered tests (e.g., the University of California–Los Angeles' English as a Second Language Placement Examination) is not granted within the same academic term. If such large numbers of students are being tested that it becomes necessary to administer the test several times over a period of a few days, inevitably some students who take the test in the first administration will request the opportunity to retake it within a few days. This should be discouraged, since some practice advantage may accrue to the repeating students.

Distribution Extremes. After a test has been scored, it is useful to look at the *distribution*, or ranking, of scores. In general, the score interpreter should place less confidence in scores at the extreme high and low ends of the distribution, that is, the scores at the top and bottom ends of the scale. This lack of

INTERPRETING TEST SCORES

confidence is due partly to the fact that there are fewer persons in those regions with whom comparison can be made. The lack of confidence may also be due to *ceiling* or *floor effects* of the test. If a test has no difficult items and sufficient time is allowed to respond to all items, scores will tend to cluster at the top, or "ceiling," of the distribution. In that region it will be difficult to distinguish one examinee from another in the ability measured. Similarly, if a test contains mostly difficult items, scores will tend to cluster at the bottom, or "floor," of the distribution. Knowledge about the ceiling or floor effects should be considered if a test is used to evaluate instructional programs or if performance cut-off scores are being set at the extremes of the distribution. For many reasons, it is best to avoid making admissions, placement, or evaluation decisions based on cut-off points set at the extremes of the scoring distribution.

Also related to the extremes of the distribution is the notion of *sample truncation*. When students are selected for admission to a given college or university on the basis of their scores on a test, the scoring distribution of accepted candidates will change in size, shape, and scoring range from the original scoring distribution from which they were selected. This is so because those students who scored below a certain standard will have been eliminated. For example, an original group of applicants might have TOEFL scores ranging from 450 to 600. If only those with TOEFL scores of 550 or above are selected, the selected group will represent a much reduced, albeit higher, range of proficiency. Such changes will have a marked effect on correlations computed for reliability or validity estimation. As a result, correlations computed for the truncated, that is, the selected, sample will usually diminish in magnitude from the correlations computed for the entire untruncated sample. One important consequence of this phenomenon is that comparative studies of test reliability and validity will tend to be biased against the test used to select the students initially—in this case, the TOEFL—since the sample will be truncated with regard to the test used for admissions, but not with regard to other tests that may not have been used for admissions decisions—for example, the American College Tests or Graduate Records Examination.

Scaling Procedure. Some available tests of communicative competence or communicative performance allow for the rating of performance on narrow scales with as few as three levels. If Level One is said to represent inability to communicate and Level Three is said to reflect native speaker-like performance, then almost every non-native speaker of English will get a rating of two. This means that there will be little differentiation among examinees and, in consequence, the ratings will be highly unreliable, since most estimates of reliability assume that the test *will* differentiate among examinees. Although this is an extreme example, it is offered to make the point that scales must be chosen with care, since the quality of the scale will affect test reliability. This problem could relate equally to scores assigned to interviews. If decisions to assign teaching assistantships were made strictly on the basis of interview ratings on such a narrow range, it is doubtful that sufficient reliable information would result to warrant the expense of using an interview in the process.

Appropriateness of Reliability Evidence. There are many different ways to estimate test reliability, and they are likely to produce differing estimates of reliability. The appropriateness of the method chosen relates to the least desirable kinds of measurement error. One type of reliability estimation, the *test-retest method*, relies on the notion that students should be ranked in the same way if they took the test a second time. Test-retest methods of reliability estimation will detect measurement error due to changes in the learner or in the testing environment, such as differing levels of fatigue, illness, anxiety, or distraction or accommodation at the testing site. *Internal consistency methods* for estimating reliability are based on the assumption that a student should perform consistently on items of similar difficulty throughout the test. Such methods will detect measurement error due to heterogeneity of the items on the test. Deviant items that fail to distinguish examinees who possess the targeted ability from those who do not will contribute to a lack of internal consistency. *Interrater methods* of reliability estimation are used in cases where different people score language performances, usually writing and speaking. These methods will detect inconsistencies among raters in the rating process.

It is important to check the user manual to determine which kinds of reliability are reported, and then to decide whether those kinds are appropriate. Precise judgments about student writing ability, for example, may require more than consensus among raters on one product but may also require consensus over time with a variety of writing tasks. Reliability estimates are also highly dependent on the number of persons in the sample under study and the range of their abilities. It is usually not enough to report a high reliability coefficient for a test, but it is also necessary to indicate the method used to estimate reliability and to describe the sample on whom the estimate was made. Only if the method and sample used are appropriate to the test application at a given user institution can confidence be placed in the reliability estimated for the purposes of that institution.

There have been a variety of important concerns related to appropriate test score interpretation. Most of them are related to the nature and extent of validity and reliability necessary for the test scores to be meaningful. It is highly important to the test developer, the college or university admissions officer, the ESL instructor, and especially to the examinee, that test scores be interpreted appropriately.

References

Abraham, R., Klein, C., and Plakans, B. 1986. Beyond SPEAK: Testing nonnative teaching assistants under classroom conditions. Paper presented at TESOL Convention, March 1986, Anaheim, CA.

Abraham, R., and Plakans, B. 1988. Evaluating a screening/training program for nonnative speaking teaching assistants. *TESOL Quarterly* 22:505–508.

Alderson, J.C. 1987. An overview of ESL/EFL testing in Britain. In J.C. Alderson, et al., 3–4.

Alderson, J.C., Krahnke, K.J., and Stansfield, C.W., eds. 1987. *Reviews of English language proficiency tests*. Washington, D.C.: Teachers of English to Speakers of Other Languages.

Bailey, K.M. 1987. Review of Test of Spoken English. In J.C. Alderson, et al., 84–86.

Barrett, R.P. 1987. The SPEAK test: Some comments by a former user. *NAFSA Newsletter* 38.7: 20–21.

_____. 1988. A tool for evaluating language proficiency of foreign TAs. Paper presented at TESOL Convention, March 1988, Chicago, IL.

Bridgeman, B., and Carlson, S. 1983. *Survey of academic writing tasks required of graduate and undergraduate foreign students*. (TOEFL Research Report 15). Princeton, NJ: Educational Testing Service.

Briggs, S.L. 1986. Report on FTA evaluations, 1985–86. (Available from the Clearinghouse on International TA Training Programs, University of Wyoming.)

The British Council. 1985. *English language requirements in British educational institutions*. London: English Language Management Department, The British Council.

The British Council. 1988. *English language entrance requirements in British educational institutions*. London: English Language Services Department, The British Council.

Brown, K.A., Fishman, P.F., and Jones, N.L. 1989. Language proficiency legislation and the international teaching assistant: An overview of legal

REFERENCES

questions. Paper presented at 41st Annual NAFSA Conference, May 1989, Minneapolis, MN.

Byrd, P. 1987. Being seduced by face validity: Linguistic and administrative issues in videotaped teaching simulation testing. In Chism, N.V., ed., *Employment and education of teaching assistants*, 355–357. Columbus, OH: Center for Teaching Excellence, The Ohio State University.

Carlson, S.B., Bridgeman, B., Camp, R., and Waanders, J. 1985. *Relationship of admission test scores to writing performance of native and nonnative speakers of English*. (TOEFL Research Report 19). Princeton, NJ: Educational Testing Service.

Carrell, P., Sarwark, S., and Plakans, B. 1987. Innovative international teaching assistant screening techniques. In Chism, N.V., ed., *Employment and education of teaching assistants*, 351–354. Columbus, OH: Center for Teaching Excellence, The Ohio State University.

Carroll, J.B., and West R. 1989. *ESU Framework*. Harlow, U.K.: Longman.

Clark, J.L.D., and Swinton, S.S. 1979. *An exploration of speaking proficiency measures in the TOEFL context*. (TOEFL Research Report 4). Princeton, NJ: Educational Testing Service.

Clark, J.L.D., and Swinton, S.S. 1980. *The test of spoken English as a measure of communicative ability in English-medium instructional settings*. (TOEFL Research Report 7). Princeton, NJ: Educational Testing Service.

Committee to Develop Standards for Educational and Psychological Testing. 1985. *Standards for educational and psychological testing*. American Educational Research Association, National CME, The American Psychological Association. Washington, D.C.: The American Psychological Association.

Constantinides, J.C. 1987. Background issues in testing and evaluation of foreign teaching assistants. In J.C. Constantinides, ed., *Papers of the Wyoming/NAFSA Institute on Foreign TA Training*, July 1986, 1:23–37. Laramie, WY: Wyoming/NAFSA Institute.

Criper, C., and Davies, A. 1988. *ELTS Validation Project Report*. ELTS Research Report I(i). London: The British Council and The University of Cambridge Local Examinations Syndicate.

Dunnett, S.C., ed., with Dubin, F., and Lezberg, A. 1980. English language teaching from an intercultural perspective. In G. Althen, ed., *Learning across cultures*, 51–71. Washington, D.C.: NAFSA.

Educational Testing Service. 1982a. *ETS oral proficiency testing manual*. Princeton, NJ: Educational Testing Service.

———. 1982b. *Test of Spoken English: Manual for score users*. Princeton, NJ: Educational Testing Service.

———. 1983. *Test of Spoken English*. Princeton, NJ: Educational Testing Service.

———. 1986. *Test of Written English Scoring Guidelines*. Princeton, NJ: Educational Testing Service.

REFERENCES

———. 1987. *TOEFL Test and Score Manual.* Princeton, NJ: Educational Testing Service.

———. 1988. *Bulletin of Information for TOEFL and TSE.* Princeton, NJ: Educational Testing Service.

———. 1989. *Test of Written English Guide.* Princeton, NJ: Educational Testing Service.

English Language Institute. 1989. *MELAB Information Bulletin.* Ann Arbor, MI: English Language Institute, University of Michigan.

Hughes, A., Porter, D., and Weir, C. 1988. ELTS validation project: Proceedings of a conference held to consider the ELTS validation project report. ELTS Research Report (ii). London: The British Council and The University of Cambridge Local Examinations Syndicate.

Jacobs, H.L., Zingraf, S.A., Wormuth, D.R., Hartfiel, V.F., and Hughey, J.B. 1981. *Testing ESL composition: A practical approach.* Rowley, MA: Newbury House.

Jenks, F. 1987. Review of Michigan Test of English Language Proficiency. In J.C. Alderson, et al., 58–60.

Johncock, P. 1988. FTA tests and university ETA testing policies. In J.C. Constantinides, ed., *Papers of the Wyoming/NAFSA Institute on Foreign TA Training,* July 1987, 2:19–38. Laramie, WY: Wyoming/NAFSA Institute.

Jones, R. 1979. Performance testing of second language proficiency. In E. Briere, and F. Hinofotis, eds., *Concepts in language testing: Some recent studies.* Washington, D.C.: Teachers of English to Speakers of Other Languages.

Jones, S. 1987. Review of Michigan Test of Aural Comprehension. In J.C. Alderson, et al., 60–61.

Lloyd-Jones, R. 1982. Skepticism about test scores. In K.L. Greenberg, H.S. Weiner, and R.A. Donovan, eds., *Notes from the National Testing Network in Writing,* 3. New York: Instructional Resource Center, City University of New York.

Madsen, H., Haskell, J., and Stansfield, C. 1988. TOEFL myths: Separating fact from fiction. Paper presented at TESOL Convention, March 1988, Chicago, IL.

Oller, J.W. 1979. *Language Tests at School.* London: Longman.

Ostler, S.E. 1980. A survey of academic needs for advanced ESL. *TESOL Quarterly* 14:489–502.

Riggles, J., and Frampton, N. 1988. The prospective international teaching assistant: A survey of evaluation procedures. Paper presented at TESOL Convention, March 1988, Chicago, IL.

Ross, J. 1988. *Report on the Test of Written English Survey: An ETS internal report to the November 1988 Meeting of the TOEFL Policy Council.* Princeton, NJ: Educational Testing Service.

Ruth, L., and Murphy, S. 1988. *Designing writing tasks for the assessment of writing.* Norwood, NJ: Ablex.

REFERENCES

Smith, R. June 1988. Orientation of American students to foreign teaching assistants. Paper presented at NAFSA Annual Conference, Washington, D.C.

Stansfield, C.W., and Ballard, R.J. 1984. Two instruments for assessing the oral English proficiency of foreign teaching assistants. In K. M. Bailey, F. Pialorsi, and J. Zukowski/Faust, eds., *Foreign teaching assistants in U.S. universities*, 101-109. Washington, D.C.: NAFSA.

Underhill, N. 1987. *Testing spoken language.* Cambridge, U.K.: Cambridge University Press.

vom Saal, D.R. 1987. The undergraduate experience and international teaching assistants. In Chism, N.V., ed., *Employment and education of teaching assistants*, 267-274. Columbus, OH: Center for Teaching Excellence, The Ohio State University.

White, R.V. 1980. *Teaching written English.* London: George Allen and Unwin.

Appendix A

Addresses for information on
English language testing:

American Council on the Teaching
 of Foreign Languages
579 Broadway
Hastings-on-Hudson, NY 10706
USA

American Language Institute
Georgetown University
Washington, DC 20057
USA

The Associated Examining Board
South Western Office
Netherton House
23-29 Marsh Street
Bristol BS1 4BP
UK

Association of Recognized English
 Language Schools
Ewert House
Ewert Place
Summertown
Oxford OX2 7BZ
UK

Center for Applied Linguistics
Division of Foreign Language
 Education and Testing
1118 22nd Street, NW
Washington, DC 20037
USA

Educational Testing Service
Princeton, NJ 08541-6161
USA

English Language Institute
Testing and Certification Division
3020 North University Building
The University of Michigan
Ann Arbor, MI 48109-1057
USA

English Language Testing Service
The British Council
10 Spring Gardens
London SW1A 2BN
UK

English Speaking Union of the
 Commonwealth
Dartmouth House
37 Charles Street
London W1X 8AB
UK

APPENDICES

Joint Matriculation Board
Manchester M15 6EU
UK

National Association for Foreign
  Student Affairs
1860 19th Street, NW
Washington, DC 20009
USA

Northwest Regional Examinations
  Board
Town Hall
Walkden Road
Worsley
Manchester M28 4QE
UK

Teachers of English to Speakers of
  Other Languages
1600 Cameron Street
Suite 300
Alexandria, VA 22314
USA

University of Cambridge Local
  Examinations Syndicate
Syndicate Buildings
1 Hills Road
Cambridge CB1 2EU
UK

University of London School
  Examinations Board
Stewart House
32 Russell Square
London WC1B 5DN
UK

University of Oxford Delegacy of
  Local Examinations
Ewert House Ewert Place
Summertown
Oxford, OX1 7BZ
UK

U.S. Government Interagency
  Language Roundtable
Box 9212
Rosslyn, VA 22209
USA

Appendix B

ESL Composition Test Questionnaire

1. Does your institution require a locally administered composition exam for the entrance or placement of international students?

   If your institution does not require a composition exam:

2. How is ESL student entrance to or placement in university courses and levels of English instruction determined?

   If your institution does require a composition exam:

3. How many students are tested each semester?
4. Approximately how many different nationalities are tested?
5. When is the composition test administered? _____ a few days/a week before the semester _____ during the first day/week of the semester _____ other: please explain.
6. Who administers the test? _____ instructor _____ departmental supervisor _____ test administrator _____ other: please explain.
7. Where is the test administered? _____ classroom _____ designated testing center _____ other: please explain.
8. How much time is allowed for the test? _____ (minutes/hours)
9. Is the writing sample _____ first draft writing _____ revised writing?
10. Is the composition administered along with other test segments such as reading, listening, etc? If so, what are they?
11. How long is the total testing session?
12. Is the writing sample taken at the _____ beginning _____ middle _____ end of the testing session?
13. What, if any, preparation by _____ instructors _____ test administrators or _____ others do students have _____ before or _____ during the test? _____ instructions _____ discussion of the prompt _____ prewriting _____ other: please explain.

APPENDICES

14. What kind(s) of prompts are used? _____ personal experience _____ mode-oriented _____ persuasive _____ other: please explain. Do students have a choice of topics? If so, how many? Do students write on more than one topic? If so, how many?
15. How was this kind of prompt selected?
16. Are these prompts field tested? If so, how?
17. Are prompts kept secure? If not, what access do students have to them?
18. Who reads and evaluates the compositions after the test?
19. When are the compositions read? _____ immediately _____ next day/week _____ other: please explain.
20. Are the compositions read by readers as a group in one location, or by individuals reading in various locations?
21. How many readers evaluate/score each composition?
22. Are readers provided with any special training? If so, briefly describe the training.
23. What means of evaluation do they use? _____ pass/fail _____ 4-, 5-, 6- point scale _____ A, B, C, D, F _____ primary-trait _____ analytic scale _____ other: please explain.
24. What constitutes a discrepancy between or among readers?
25. How are discrepancies resolved? _____ third reader _____ fourth reader. Who serves as the resolution reader?
26. What kind of score is reported? _____ a single whole score _____ other: please explain.
27. Does the score report include any specific commentary? If so, how is it used?
28. How does the evaluation of compositions account for "off topic" or "no response" papers?
29. How are the results of the composition exam used? _____ entrance _____ placement _____ exit _____ other: please explain.
30. Please include any other information that you think is pertinent to the local administration and use of your composition test:

98